The Graham Formula

S+C+F=D(.25)=B

Why most decisions for Christ are ineffective

Patrick McIntyre

The Graham Formula
White Harvest Publishing
9967 Hwy 9, Mammoth Spring, AR 72554
www.christianebooks.com, www.sfee.info

ISBN 0-9635050-2-5 Copyright 2005 by Patrick McIntyre
Scripture quotations are taken from the King James Version unless noted otherwise
Other books by Patrick McIntyre: *Intimacy With God*

Cover Photo: Digital Vision/Getty Images

It happened one night...

In one of Jesus' parables, He tells the story of a feast. A man sent out many invitations to a great feast he was planning. Many of the guests, however, gave excuses and refused to attend. A pastor asked the Bible study group he was teaching, "What did God mean when He said, 'None of those men which were bidden shall taste of my supper' (Luke 14:24)?" The group discussed several ideas, not coming to any real conclusion. Then someone read the same parable in Matthew. This version of the parable ends by saying, "Many are called, but few are chosen" (Matthew 22:14). All agreed that the people who didn't come to the supper were lost–without Christ.

The pastor continued, "Jesus must have seen shock in the eyes of the multitude He was teaching, for He quickly added more illustrations: 'If any man come to me, and hate not his father, and mother, and wife, and children, and brethren, and sisters, yea, and his own life also, he cannot be my disciple. ... For which of you, intending to build a tower, sitteth not down first, and counteth the cost, whether he have sufficient to finish it? ... whosoever he be of you that forsaketh not *all* that he hath, he cannot be my disciple'" (Luke 14:26-33).

"But wait a second, Pastor," said a teenager. "Isn't Jesus speaking about disciples here? He's not talking about people like us. ... He's talking about *disciples**."

The group sat quietly. Then one of the young men exclaimed, "Did Jesus say regular Christians are disciples? If that's so, *none* of my friends are saved!"

The pastor struggled for an answer. He didn't have the heart to tell him the truth.

---

* In the four Gospels, the word translated "disciple" is the word used most to describe followers of Jesus (Luke 19:37). If you weren't a disciple, you couldn't be considered a "Christian" in any sense. All the people Jesus and the apostles baptized were called disciples (John 4:1). In the book of Acts, all the people who joined the church were called disciples (Acts 6:1-2). It was later that disciples were called Christians (Acts 11:26). The word *Christian* is used only three times in the Bible. In most cases, followers of Christ were called disciples (262 times) or saints (62 times).

Early in Billy Graham's career ... he realized that most decisions for Christ were ineffective if they were the result of a sermon alone. He said getting a decision was only 5% of the work... that counseling and follow-up were absolutely essential. He developed a three-part formula for success.

Sermon + Counseling + Follow-up = effective decisions

But despite his best efforts, he noticed that just 25% of the decisions for Christ made at crusades were effective.[1]

$$S+C+F=D(.25)=B$$

This is the Graham Formula

S=Sermon, C=Counseling, F=Follow-up, D=Decisions, B=Born Again Experience

Unfortunately, most evangelical ministers employ only one third of the Graham Formula without offering counseling and follow-up. This timesaving practice has resulted in even more spurious conversions.

Spurious Conversions Affect Everyone

Twelve years after making a decision for Christ, Franklin Graham needed to be born again.[2] He was angry and confused when his father told him the truth, but God granted him repentance, new life, and a wonderful ministry. Praise God that Billy Graham had enough tough love to put *both* their reputations on the line. This book was written to help you do the same for your loved ones.

1. "Reverend Billy Graham talking with David Frost," PBS, January 23, 1993 as recorded in David Frost's *Billy Graham - Personal Thoughts of a Public Man,* (1997), pp.71-72
2. Franklin Graham, *Rebel With A Cause,* (1995), p.120

Dedication

This book is dedicated to Charles Finney, the father of the altar call, and Billy Graham, the father of the group salvation prayer. In the first half of the 1800s, Finney began using methods designed to encourage seekers to immediately confront their lost condition. After a church service, he asked seekers to come to an after-meeting or inquiry room where they could confess their sins, receive counsel and be prayed for. Many pastors thought this practice was confusing, giving the impression that one could be saved by an external act. In the nineteenth century, salvation was seen as dependent on the sovereignty of God. Asking someone to do something in order to be saved was considered presumptuous at best.

Although Finney's after-meeting was the forerunner of today's altar call, the purpose was not merely to get people to make a decision for Christ. Rather, it was the means by which the inquirer could receive additional instruction about repentance and the means of grace while waiting on God for the gift of salvation.

Unfortunately, lesser men used Finney's methods without the safeguard of extensive counseling. Within seventy-five years, as liberal theology crept into churches, salvation was seen less as a Holy Spirit birth (John 3:8), and more as a decision of the will.

Then, in the early 1900s, Billy Sunday popularized the idea that everyone who came forward in an altar call was no longer just an inquirer, but a convert. He eliminated the inquiry room and no longer offered pre-salvation counseling.

Fifty years later, Billy Graham saw the problems caused by Sunday's mistake and brought back the inquiry room and began vigorous counseling and follow-up programs to minimize spurious conversions. Unfortunately, as the crowds grew larger, he began to use a new time-saving device: the group salvation prayer. This innovation was never intended to be used apart from the safeguards. History has repeated itself. What Sunday did to Finney's methods, so evangelical ministers have done to Graham's formula for success, turning it into a recipe for disaster.

Definitions of words used in this book

antinomianism: Heretical belief that faith in Christ frees the Christian from obligation to observe moral law, especially the Ten Commandments.

Arminian: Someone who believes that people have a significant influence over whether or not they are born again, and believes that born-again Christians can lose their salvation.

born-again experience: A spiritual birth which transforms someone into a true Christian, a saint, by the activity of the Holy Spirit. See Matthew 3:11; John 3:3-8; 7:39; 14:17; 20:22; Acts 2:38; Romans 8:2-26; 14:17; 1 Corinthians 2:10-12; 3:16; 6:11-19; 12:13; 2 Corinthians 3:3; 17-18; Galatians 3:2-5, 14; 4:6; Ephesians 1:13; 3:16; 4:30; 5:18; Philippians 2:1; 1 Thessalonians 4:8; 2 Thessalonians 2:13; 2 Timothy 1:14; Titus 3:5; Hebrews 6:4; 1 Peter 1:2,22; 1 John 3:24; 4:13; Jude 1:20.

Calvinist: Someone who believes that people have little influence over whether or not they will be born again and that born-again Christians cannot lose their salvation.

evangelical: Someone who is *supposed* to believe in the sole authority and inerrancy of the Bible; in salvation only through regeneration, the born again experience and in a spiritually transformed personal life.

Evangelical (large E): A true Christian, a saint, as described by George Barna for statistical purposes (see pages 21-24).

forensic salvation: The legal standing of innocence before God apart from discernible evidence of salvation wrought by the activity of the Holy Spirit within a saint.

Gnostic Christianity: Heretical belief system characterized by the supposed forensic salvation of someone in the spiritual realm without any discernible evidence of salvation worked in the physical realm. Some proponents of early Gnosticism adopted a form of antinomianism in sexual matters, holding that people are accountable only in matters of the spirit.

holistic salvation: Forensic salvation plus the expectation of discernible evidence of salvation wrought by the activity of the Holy Spirit within a saint.

Contents:

Dedication..........5
Definitions..........6
Introduction..........8
The Front Page..........11
The Faith System..........14
General Hospital..........21
A Funny Thing Happened on the way to the Temple..........25
The Hour of Decision..........31
Edwards, Whitefield and Wesley..........34
Charles Finney..........39
Billy Sunday Changes Everything..........44
Billy Sunday Evangelism Evolves..........51
The Billy Graham Formula..........64
The Evangelical Sacrament..........74
Billy Sunday Evangelism Hits the Fan..........76
The Bride of Christ..........82
The Two Yardsticks of Salvation..........88
What do you think I am, a Saint?..........92
What does it mean to "Believe on the Lord Jesus Christ"?..........97
Church People Get Saved..........105
A Call to Action..........107
Footnotes..........108

Appendices
A. Evangelism Timeline..........113
B. Two Doctrines that Helped effective evangelism..........114
C. Wesley's Waiting on God for Salvation..........117
From the works of Charles Finney:
D. False Comfort for Sinners..........118
E. Directions to Sinners..........121
F. True and False conversions..........122
G. About the Author..........125

Introduction

Dr. James Dobson, founder of the powerful and influential Christian ministry, Focus on the Family, added a postscript to a letter sent to members. "A brand new Gallup Poll was released this week. ... According to the latest survey, 74 percent of Americans indicated they have made a personal commitment to Jesus Christ, compared to 66 percent in 1988 and 60 percent in 1978! Ninety-five percent of those professing a relationship with Christ were willing to call it a 'born-again' experience."[1] Pretty impressive ... until you realize this letter was written in 1990.

After fifteen years of moral decline unprecedented in American history, these glowing statistics indicated only one thing ... things were not what they seemed. However, Dobson gives us an insight into how to make sense of the amazing statistics. "Even if only half of these are what might be considered valid spiritual commitments (only God knows), the number is still encouraging."[2]

Those twenty-two words contain the problem in a nutshell. While rejoicing that perhaps 74 percent of Americans are saved, he casually acknowledges the possibility that half of them could be deceived. This blasé attitude would be acceptable if he was talking about how many Americans believe in God or think they're basically good, but he's referring to people who believe they are going to heaven because they said a salvation prayer. And to make matters worse, most of these people believe there is no way they can lose their salvation no matter how they live their lives. According to Barna Research Group, these unfortunate individuals make up most of evangelical Christianity in America.[3]

No wonder the Christian Right movement is a mile wide, but only an inch deep; why the majority of Americans think they're Christian while they act like heathen; why 88% of the children raised in evangelical homes leave church at the age of 18, never to return; why the divorce rate of evangelical church members is virtually the same as the general population. [4]

The scandal of modern evangelism isn't a scandal like Watergate--it's *much* more serious. In this scandal, people don't go to prison; they go to hell.

Are we fulfilling the Great Commission or just fooling ourselves? Billy Graham said that perhaps only a fourth of the decisions made at his crusades, including those who receive counseling and long-term follow-up, result in people being born again.[5] But modern evangelism theology dictates that we tell everyone who repeats a salvation prayer they are saved. This deplorable practice has become commonplace in most evangelical churches, giving the vast majority of those who walk away from the altar a false sense of security.

When Christianity was legalized in fourth century Rome, the number of proclaimed Christians grew from 10 percent to over 90 percent of the population in fewer than 100 years[6] due to admitting heathen who were willing to perform a symbolic act. The fact that churches were watered down by worldliness was looked on as a necessary evil in the interest of survival and expansion of the faith. As a result, Christianity became the establishment religion during the most decadent period of Roman history.

A similar condition exists today in America. Since the 1950s, the number of evangelicals has increased in proportion to the use of the salvation prayer system. We are now the establishment religion, but at what cost? The decline of evangelical holiness has left us unable to stop the moral freefall of our society. Most pastors have a "don't ask, don't tell" policy toward sin in their congregations.

Dr. Rod Bell, president of the Fundamentalist Baptist Fellowship of America, believes 50 percent of people that go to church are lost.[7] Evangelist Luis Palau said of the 80 percent of Americans who claim to be Christian, "Few live any differently from pagans or atheists, as though God has no claim on their lives."[8] Dr. James Dobson admitted, "The majority of Americans are dabbling in religious expression that has no substance."[9]

Bill Bright said, "... many who call themselves Christians are not really biblical Christians at all. Although they may be religious people who attend church regularly, they have never experienced the new birth and a personal relationship with Jesus Christ."[10]

Bright blamed our "backslidden" state on a lack of "sanctification." As you learn about modern evangelism, you'll see the obvious truth. One hundred years ago, evangelists were ecstatic if 10 percent of the people who came forward for altar calls were born again. Today, a 100 percent success rate is assumed. Either we've improved the way we deliver the Gospel, or our methods are producing a staggering number of stillbirths.

And we're exporting our methods. I've sat through more than a few missionary presentations in which I was expected to believe village natives who had never before heard the Gospel all got saved after a single sermon. How different this is from the experience of missionaries before the twentieth century! Adoniram Judson, America's first foreign missionary to India, worked for seven years before gaining his first converts. David Livingstone, missionary to Africa, worked four years before anyone was saved. William Carey, British missionary to India, worked seven years before he saw his first salvation. Even today, when native missionaries labor for the lost in untouched Indian villages, one or two converts the first year are considered very good. But send an American evangelist to that same village with the *Jesus* film and *everyone* gets saved!

The Front Page

On the twentieth floor of the Hancock Building, the Christian magazine publisher looked down at the street from his penthouse office. On his mahogany desk was a pile of books and periodicals. To his right were a coffee table and three armless chairs. In the middle chair sat an attractive blonde.

The city was alive with rush hour traffic. The pedestrians reminded him of insects, moving in random patterns. He muttered under his breath, "They look like ants."

"Did you say something, boss?" The young reporter looked up with eager eyes. Her boss didn't look at her. He hated having to tell her the bad news.

"No. … Now, about this article of yours, it's too controversial. We can't print it." He stared out the window again. "I'm sorry."

"Why can't you print it? I've documented every fact. The key subjects are all on record and there's no way we can be sued."

"Listen , your source says that 90 percent of Americans who said a salvation prayer aren't really saved.[1] That's just too far out. I don't want those kind of statements linked in any way to our magazine."

"My source happens to be the most famous street evangelist in history. He's published numerous books, been endorsed by big name ministries, has a massive following and does a TV show with a movie star."

"Yeah? Well he's not big enough to take on the evangelical establishment! I'm sorry. If we publish your article, they could break us ... just like that!" He slammed his hand on the table for effect. "Where do you think we get the advertising dollars that pays your salary?"

"But this is a bigger scandal than Jimmy Swaggart and Jim Baker put together! I mean–millions of people who think they're saved are going to hell!"

"Let's not talk about it! I'm not going to jeopardize this magazine for the sake of what may or may not happen to people after they die!"

This scene could have taken place if an investigative reporter wrote an article on the shocking data presented in *The Way of the Master* by Ray Comfort. Here's a sample:

* At a 1990 crusade in the United States, 600 decisions for Christ were recorded ... three months later, a follow-up was done, and not even one of the inquirers was continuing in their faith.

* In 1985, a four day crusade obtained 217 decisions for Christ. Research indicated that 92 percent fell away.

* Charles E Hackett, the Assemblies of God Home Missions National Director for the United States, said, "A soul at the altar does not generate much excitement in some circles because we realize approximately ninety-five out of a hundred will not become integrated into the church. In fact, most of them will not return for a second visit."

* A missionary team from Boulder, Colorado, went to Russia in 1991 and obtained 2,500 decisions for Christ. The next year, the team went back and found only thirty continuing in their faith.

* In 1970, local churches cooperated in a Fort Worth, Texas event and obtained 30,000 decisions for Christ. Six months later, follow-up revealed only thirty continuing in their faith.

* A crusade reported by *Church Growth* magazine boasted of 18,000 decisions for Christ, but the article went on to admit that only 6 percent of the "converts" were incorporated into a local church.

* In 1995, a leading U.S. denomination reported 384,057 decisions for Christ, but only 22,983 were in fellowship a short time later. Ninety-four percent couldn't be accounted for.

* A pastor of a large church in Omaha, Nebraska, said he was involved with a crusade where 1,300 decisions were made, yet not even one "convert" continued in his or her faith.

Statistics consistently showing an 84 to 97 percent fall-away rate are not confined to crusades, but are typical throughout local church evangelism.[2]

Why Listen to Ray Comfort?

Street evangelists are the sergeants of evangelism. While parachurch ministries typically tell others how to evangelize, street evangelists see the battle firsthand. The war looks very different on the ground. Others may study maps and give orders, but street evangelists fight hand-to-hand combat. In other words, Comfort *knows* what's going on out there.

Unlike other influential people in the evangelical establishment, he is willing to question the misleading numbers of high-profile ministries.

The Emperor's New Clothes

Pastors acknowledge privately that many decisions for Christ are ineffective, but in order to maintain confidence in the system, never say so publicly. Every time a missionary says "X amount got saved," other missionaries know only a portion were truly born again. But the general public makes no such distinction. They either believe us with superstitious reverence, being too afraid or too trusting to question the system, or they don't care.

It's scary—and Jesus said we would be held accountable for every idle word. What will our reward be for telling people they're saved when they're not?

A non-stop party keeps us intoxicated with self congratulations, judging ourselves by ourselves (2 Corinthians 10:12). Someday a little boy will wander into the evangelical palace. We won't notice him when he walks into our celebration with a shocked look on his face until he points at us and says, "You're naked" (Revelation 3:17).

The Faith System

Before Billy Sunday introduced the idea that everyone who came forward in an altar call was a convert, the parable of the seed (Matthew 13:18-23) taught most people would receive the Gospel with joy, but, if their hearts were not right, they would not be saved. The parable of the tares (Matthew 13:24-30) taught the difference between false converts and saints—regardless of outward appearances and how the enemy would try to use those tares to destroy the church. But now it seems modern science has overcome the deficiencies of the human heart and defeated the devil as well.

Once Upon a Time...

In the Cumberland Valley, on opposite sides of the road leading into town, there were two farms with identical soil and terrain. For twelve generations, the two families were content to produce twenty-five bushels of wheat per acre. They worked hard, fertilizing and tilling the soil in the spring, protecting the crop from birds and insects during the growing season and carefully separating the tares from the wheat at harvest time. Using the methods of their fathers, they kept the seed free from tares.

Then, in 1918, one of the farmers read in *Free Thinker* magazine about a new way to assure a higher yield of wheat without the fuss of using extra fertilizer, tilling or picking off insects. One of the great advantages of the system over traditional methods was it guaranteed tares would no longer be a problem ... because tares could now be treated as wheat. The theory was if you ignored the tares, they would eventually become wheat, thus increasing the yield.

It was called the Faith System. This system guaranteed that every seed would produce a healthy stalk of wheat, resulting in at least one hundred bushels per acre. The only requirement was the farmers must encourage the soil to believe it was capable of producing fruit from every seed. *Free Thinker* listed a few tried and true slogans to tell the soil. "Believe you can produce fruit from every seed!" and "Believe and you will produce!" were the most popular.

The words of the slogans were not as important as the way they were spoken. *Free Thinker* suggested perhaps just yelling the word "believe" over and over again would have the same result, and the more emotional the delivery, the better. For this reason, some farmers employed out-of-work Shakespearian actors to address the fields. "To believe or not to be believe, that is the question ... believe!" could be heard day and night on the more progressive farms.

The farmer put down the *Free Thinker* magazine and decided to put the Faith System to the test. He hired an unemployed Shakespearian actor to encourage his fields. That first year, the fields seemed more full of wheat than ever. When reaping time came, the tares were harvested along with the wheat. Since there was no separating (every year before, tares were burned so as not to contaminate the wheat), the seed for next year's planting was a mixture of wheat and tares. The seed mixture did wonderfully, and since tares have few natural enemies and grow more vigorously than wheat, within twenty years the Faith System was producing one hundred bushels per acre. (The fact that it was mostly tares was irrelevant. Although the new type of wheat had almost no nutrition, and the bread made from it was unhealthy, this was a small price to pay for such a fantastic yield.)

The farmer across the road didn't adopt the Faith System and continued to produce only twenty-five bushels of wheat per acre. He didn't begrudge his neighbor and never complained about having to burn more tares than ever before (wind blew the seed across the road), but he dreaded going into town, for when he went to the general store, sometimes people would point at him and say, "See how foolish that fellow is. He only produces twenty-five bushels of wheat per acre!"

Jesus used many parables to illustrate why so few people get saved. Whether he spoke of seeds, tares or the leaven of the Pharisees, the message was clear: You can't save more people by lowering the standards of the Gospel. The Faith System removed the biblical requirements of true repentance and water baptism and replaced them with a simplistic understanding of Romans 10:9: "That if thou shalt confess with thy mouth the Lord Jesus, and shalt believe in thine heart that God hath raised him from the dead, thou shalt be saved."

More will be said on this subject later, but for now, let's just agree with James (James 2:19), that even devils could be saved if the definition of saving faith is just believing in God. The result of the Faith System is millions of tares have been told they are born again, effectively lowering the expectation of Christian morality. The Faith System grew from a man-centered psychological paradigm that teaches faith is just another word for having hope that God has removed the penalty for sin, and repentance is just another word for being sorry for being a sinner.

The Faith System depends on the mind-set of the person you're trying to save. The main objective is to get the penitent to make a commitment to Christ and then convince him he is saved as the result. Most pastors and evangelists assume it's always God's will to save every lost person who comes to the altar, regardless of their specific needs at the time. In fact, counselors at some events are trained to keep "on track" at all costs and consider legitimate reservations of inquirers to be diversions from the purpose of getting them saved.

Counselors are taught to tell inquirers, "Don't believe your feelings; believe the Word of God." They're understandably concerned that most inquirers have no internal witness that anything has changed; for most, nothing has. The Word of God in this case replaces God as the focus of trust. It is no longer necessary to have supernatural faith from God, which is the substance of things hoped for, the evidence of things not seen (Hebrews 11:1). If you have no substance and no evidence, all you have left is a natural faith—which is really hope—in the Word of God.

How did the definition of saving faith evolve? According to John Dillenberger and Claude Welch, "A terrible inversion had taken place. Religion had been substituted for God. The process was similar to the later development of Lutherism, in which the doctrine of justification by faith in God had been subtly transformed into faith in faith itself, i.e., into a confidence in the saving power of faith rather than the God of faith. Now liberalism had fallen before the same temptation by putting the emphasis on religion rather than God ... 'inversion of faith whereby man puts himself into the center, constructs an anthropocentric universe and makes confidence in his own value rather than faith in God in the beginning.'"[1]

Trusting in God's Word for salvation has replaced trusting in God for salvation for the same reason trusting in God's Word for healing and prosperity has become popular. According to the new faith theology, God has to provide salvation, healing and prosperity as soon as the enlightened person demands it "by faith." Of course, this makes the obtaining of salvation much easier on the minister because the specific will of God for the individual is no longer uncertain.

But this man-centered theology makes sense only if God doesn't meddle in the process. An omniscient, *personal* God is no longer needed or welcome. For the Faith System to work, God *must* distribute salvation equally and without prejudice. He must turn a blind eye to the specific needs of individuals and their circle of influence. *Everyone* who says the prayer with sincerity *must* be born-again for the System to work. That's why "believing you're saved" is so important.

A Reason For Using Psychology

Modern psychology has taught us if a man believes he is good-looking, he is likely to be more self-assured and confident. Therefore, it makes sense that, if a man thinks he is loved by God, he is more likely to act like a Christian. The only problem with this psychological paradigm is, if you convince a lost person he's saved, he is *less* likely to seek salvation, and just acting like a saint doesn't make you one. In fact, up until the twentieth century, evangelicals spent the bulk of their time convincing moral and religious people they needed to get saved. Today the pendulum has swung to the opposite side. Now we try to convince people who've said a salvation prayer but are unsure of their salvation they are the apple of God's eye.

Whatever Happened to the Sovereignty of God?

Contrary to popular opinion, it's ultimately up to God when and how He saves someone. At least this was the understanding of almost all evangelicals before the twentieth century. Listen to the famous Arminian evangelist, John Wesley: "Holy faith is the gift of God; and he is never straitened for time. He can as easily give this faith in a moment as in a thousand years. He frequently does give it on a death-bed, in answer to the prayer of believers, but rarely, if ever, to those who had continued unholy, upon the presumption that He would save them at last."[2]

"We know not why he bestows this on some even before they ask for it (some unquestionable instances of which we have seen); on some after they have sought it but a few days: and permits other believers [a believer is this case is someone who seeks salvation, but who is not yet born again] to wait for it, perhaps twenty, thirty, or forty years; nay, and others till a few hours, or even minutes, before their spirits return to him [Wesley speaks of physical death]."[3]

Before the twentieth century, most evangelical pastors and evangelists understood the difference between those God had saved and those who merely had made a "profession of faith." This is what set evangelicals apart from the majority of American Christians.

Evangelicals were called "Bible thumpers" because they refused to compromise the born-again standard. Before the twentieth century, evangelists and pastors encouraged believers who weren't yet born again to use the "means of grace" as they waited on God for salvation. (See Appendix C.) Today, there's no more waiting at the altar. Salvation is guaranteed if you just "repeat after me ..."

Franklin Graham Gets Saved

Franklin Graham, the son of the famous evangelist, is a good example of someone who was confused by modern theology. When he made a decision for Christ at age eight, he assumed he was saved, but his parents knew from his attitude and behavior he wasn't born again. The time came in 1974 when his father told him, "You're going to have to make a choice either to accept Christ or reject Him. You can't continue to play the middle ground. Either you are going to choose to follow and obey Him or reject Him."[4]

Franklin was twenty-two years old. It had been fourteen years since he made his decision for Christ. But he knew deep down that something wasn't right. "I felt I was a Christian. ... I found myself talking as though there were two people struggling inside of me."[5] Franklin didn't know it, but his struggle of faith was a typical example of what happens when someone is illuminated by the Holy Spirit before repenting.

"I thought back to the time I made a decision for Christ at age eight. I'm not sure I really understood what I had done. ... All I knew was that I wanted the big empty hole inside of me to be filled. ... I read Romans 8:1 over and over, and realized that I was not 'in' Christ. More than anything else, I wanted to be, but didn't know how."[6] That night, Franklin Graham repented and God saved him. He was born again.

Assuring Everyone They're Saved

As mentioned earlier, Billy Graham, the most famous modern evangelist, believes only a portion of the people who come to the altar are saved at that moment.[7] For this reason, the Graham organization considers their efforts to be "little more than a mass movement, a crowd following a crowd, a wave of religious emotion which quickly evaporated,"[8] if not accompanied with competent counseling[9] and concerted follow-up.[10]

Since modern evangelism doesn't require water baptism with all it entails and church attendance with the possibility of further instruction, the vast majority of people who say a formula salvation prayer are like seeds that die for lack of soil (Matthew 13:21).

When many pastors and evangelists tell people who've come forward in altar calls they're saved, they do so in the hope that God will save them sometime in the future. But some unregenerate sinners assume from this message they've got everything they need. It's like handing a teenage boy a condom and then asking him not to engage in sex. The Christian condom is telling seekers they are protected from hell no matter how they live their lives. It's like telling an AIDS patient he doesn't have the disease. Not only will he die a horrible death, but he'll most likely infect many others along the way.

Despite the fact that 83 percent of Protestant pastors describe their churches as evangelical,[11] many congregations are morally no different than heathen. American evangelical Christianity is in a lukewarm state for which revival seems unlikely. After one hundred years of automatic salvation for all who come to the altar, we've lost the desire—and the ability—to determine if people are truly Christian.

If a sustainable revival is ever to come to America, we'll need to return to pre-twentieth century standards. We must teach the fear of the Lord, the knowledge of God's sovereignty, the expectation of holiness in saints and reliance on the workings of the Holy Spirit.

Scriptural and historical facts are irrefutable. In preparing to write this book, I've read hundreds of descriptions of born-again conversions from the first to the twentieth centuries. The similarities were striking. When one realizes these saints came from many different cultures over a period of almost 2,000 years without knowing what others had experienced, the conclusion is obvious: The born-again experience is not a mere state of mind—it's a miracle!

General Hospital

Dr. George Barna, a physician attending to the American Church, stands over his patient. He looks down at her slender body. She is asleep, not aware that he has just taken a thermometer from her lips. Her face has wrinkles, showing her age, but beneath the lines is an attractive woman. He knows she is not fully aware of her sickness. She only submitted to the tests to prove she was healthy.

The doctor wonders how he can tell her the truth without destroying their relationship. Perhaps she will reject his prognosis and claim he is only trying to scare up business. He looks at the thermometer and shakes his head. The nurse looks at him expectantly (she has relatives in the church). Her quivering voice breaks the silence, "Doctor ... is it?"

"Yes, nurse. My tests are conclusive. The patient has use of only 10 percent of her vital organs. Her body is racked with cancer."

"But how is that possible? She seems so healthy. Church attendance is up from last year, 43 percent of Americans go to church, and 84 percent of Americans want to be identified as 'Christian.' So that means evangelists are doing a good job, doesn't it?"

"Yes, nurse, it all looks good on the outside, which makes it all the harder to tell her the truth. Perhaps the most disturbing fact is 83 percent of Protestant pastors describe their congregations as evangelical and conservative. That looks good on paper. But my tests show conclusively only 10 percent of American Protestants really are evangelical, and that's only 5 percent to 8 percent of Americans."

"But doctor, what does it all mean?"

"It means we've got a very sick woman on our hands. Not only is she sick, but, because she thinks she's healthy, she keeps doing the things that make her sick." The doctor's face turns red as he suddenly grabs the woman's shoulders. "I'd like to wake her up and knock some sense into her!"

"Doctor, control yourself!"

"I'm sorry, nurse; that's what I'd like to do. But how do I

make her see she needs to completely change her way of life?"

This scene at General Hospital could have taken place when George Barna released his book, *State of the Church 2002*. Barna had been tracking church decline for almost twenty years. His *State of the Church 2002* was a scathing expose of the church in America. Church leaders have long relied on Barna to provide independent analysis on the health of the American church. His perspective is the result of empirical data, not just subjective analysis. We would do well to heed his voice in the wilderness.

Here's a snapshot from his book: It's likely that the vast majority of Americans have responded at least once to an evangelist's plea for them to repeat a salvation prayer. According to a recent poll, 65 percent of Americans believe they "have made a commitment to Jesus Christ that is still important in their life."[1] (It sounds as if they've repeated a formula "salvation prayer" and consider it to be still in effect.)

Notional Christians

Barna calls 37 percent of Americans who are Christian in name only[2] "notional Christians." Members of this group do not see Jesus Christ as the reason they will go to heaven.

Born-Again Christians

Barna puts 35 percent of Americans in the 'born-again Christian" category only for statistical reasons. In order to be called "born again,"[3] they must agree with only two doctrinal statements: (1) They have made a commitment to Jesus Christ that is still important in their lives today, and (2) after they die, they will go to heaven because they have confessed their sins and accepted Jesus Christ as their Savior. Despite people's ability to choose the correct doctrinal statements, Barna considers the vast majority of this group to actually be notional Christians. He gives us the benefit of almost twenty years of objective research when he says, "Our research shows that few 'born again' Christians, despite having some appropriate doctrinal notions and having said the prerequisite prayer, never experienced the deep spiritual brokenness that enabled them to realize Jesus Christ was, is and will forever be their only hope of experiencing genuine meaning, purpose and salvation. Instead of broken people eternally grateful for the sacrifice and grace extended to them, we have millions of people who have simply tried to exploit God—people for whom salvation is little more than a fire insurance policy they won't think about until the Devil comes knockin'. In the interim we witness a 'born again' population that is indistinguishable from the rest of the nation—and has very limited credibility when it comes to promoting genuine Christianity."[4]

Later in the same chapter, Barna says of this group: "When do we get to the point at which we accept smaller numbers of intensely devoted people rather than feverishly investing in filling auditoriums and stadiums with massive numbers of the lukewarm 'Christians' that Jesus promised to spew out of His mouth (Revelation 3:16)? What might cause us to acknowledge that, yes, faith in God is good, but even the demons believe in God–and it takes more than a naïve, inch-deep faith in Christ to become part of a Church that truly honors God?"[5]

Evangelical Christians

Barna calls a third, much smaller group, "Evangelical Christians." These are the only Christians we can confidently say are most likely saved.[6] Although they make up only 5 percent to 8 percent of the population of America, they stand out as the biblical remnant who holds back the judgment of God (Genesis 18:32). They are interspersed throughout the churches. Interestingly, most Protestant pastors (83 percent)[7] describe their churches as "evangelical," while the majority of their members have no similarity to historical evangelicals.[8]

In order to be statistically called evangelical Christians, they need to agree with nine doctrinal statements:

1. They have made a commitment to Jesus Christ that is still important in their lives today.

2. They believe after they die they will go to heaven because they have confessed their sins and accepted Jesus Christ as their savior.

3. They believe in God, as described in the Bible.

4. They believe in Jesus' sinless life.

5. They believe the Bible is accurate.

6. They believe in the existence of Satan.

7. They believe in salvation by grace alone.

8. They accept personal responsibility for evangelism.

9. They say their religious faith is very important in their life today.

If someone agrees with these statements, it doesn't necessarily mean he or she is born again. But if someone doesn't agree with these statements, it's a pretty good indication he or she is not.

Only 5 to 8 percent of Americans agree with these doctrinal statements, and the numbers are falling. This is the core group who make up American biblical Christianity.

Concerning this group, Barna warns, "Whether you like them or not, the reality is that the declining numbers of evangelicals reflect a deterioration of Bible-based faith in America. Say what you will about evangelicals and their goals, their demise signals the rise of postmodernism within the Church itself."[9]

The bottom line: Barna considers only 5 to 8 percent of Americans to be truly evangelical. These are the only ones we can confidently say are most likely Christian.

American pastors are understandably concerned about the "backslidden" state of the church. But the greater issue is the millions of precious souls who are being lost to hell. The common prognosis is that the church needs to be taught how to be Christian. But the most pressing problem with the church is not a lack of sanctification, but rather, a lack of Christians.

A Funny Thing Happened on the way to the Temple

Jude and Timothy were on their way to Jerusalem for the Feast of Pentecost. As they sat at Jacob's Well, a popular pilgrim hangout, Jude saw a group of Essenes and asked, "I wonder what happened to *his* disciples?"

"Whose disciples?" asked Timothy.

"Jesus of Nazareth. It's been over forty days and I've heard rumors everywhere that he's alive, but where are the men and women who were with him?"

"I don't know. Hiding from the chief priests I guess. After what they did to him, who could blame them? You know, it was the chief priests who gave him to the Romans. I saw the whole thing."

"What? You were there when he died?"

"Yes."

Both men tried not to appear anxious. Finally, Jude spoke. "Have you heard ... he's alive?"

Again, silence. Both men were reluctant to say anything more for fear the other would suspect he was a disciple. (The chief priests had many spies.) Just then, they heard the sound of a camel driver and looked up to see a caravan winding its way down the hill.

After staring at the sight for a minute, Jude spoke. "A man in Bethel told me over 500 people saw him alive, and they're apparently telling everyone because I heard the same story in Jericho and Samaria. Do you think these people are making it up?"

More silence. Timothy chose his words carefully. "I think they *believe* they saw him. What do you think?"

"I don't know."

Both men had seen Jesus personally and knew some who were healed or had demons cast out. They understood why the religious establishment had him killed. Jesus said the righteousness of the scribes and Pharisees wasn't enough to enter the kingdom of heaven, that only the Messiah could help people change—and (the words were almost unthinkable) He, Jesus, was the Messiah.

Jude and Timothy continued on to Jerusalem and went to the temple. After the ceremony, they decided to eat at a restaurant in the Arab quarter. On the way there, a man suddenly ran past them—then another and another. Soon they were caught up in a human wave, pushing them down narrow streets till they stood at the back of a large crowd.

Jude started to ask a man what was happening when a woman put a finger to her lips and pointed at a man on a rooftop. He was yelling, "Ye men of Israel, hear these words; Jesus of Nazareth, a man approved of God among you by miracles and wonders and signs, which God did by him in the midst of you, as ye yourselves also know. Him, being delivered by the determinate counsel and foreknowledge of God, ye have taken, and by wicked hands have crucified and slain."

Jude looked at Timothy. Both knew this was the *real* reason God brought them to Jerusalem. The disciple called Peter explained how Jesus' crucifixion was the fulfillment of prophecy, and the last days were upon them. He told how God had exalted this Jesus, giving Him authority and the promise of the Holy Spirit, which He gives to all who believe in Him.

By the end of the sermon, Jude and Timothy were ready to give their lives to God. When Peter said, "Repent, and be baptized every one of you in the name of Jesus Christ for the remission of sins, and ye shall receive the gift of the Holy Ghost," they made their way forward.

Jude and Timothy were among 3,000 people the Holy Spirit prepared and drew precisely for that moment. If the 500 people (1 Corinthians 15:6) who saw Jesus alive after his resurrection told just two people a day of the experience, and those two people told two other people a day, and so on, within two weeks, everyone in Israel could have heard the good news. In fact, in the forty-seven days leading up to Pentecost, it is statistically possible that the resurrection "rumor" was shared over seven billion times.

What Kind of People Were Added to the Church?

"Then they that gladly received his word were baptized: and the same day there were added unto them about three thousand souls. And they continued steadfastly in the apostles' doctrine and fellowship, and in breaking of bread, and in prayers" (Acts 2:41-42).

This is one of the few places in the New Testament in which a large group of people was joined to the church. What was it about this group of people that enabled so many of them to give up everything and follow Jesus?

1. They were devout (Acts 2:5), already trying to please God and keep the Law. Because they were Jews or proselytes, they understood the reason for sacrifice and what repentance meant.

2. They saw how the crucifixion related specifically to them.

3. They most likely understood the meaning of water baptism, how the remission of sin was predicated on true repentance, and water baptism was a symbol of the old person dying so a new person could live.

4. They probably knew "believing on Jesus" meant a clean break with the past. Jesus had warned repeatedly that people needed to count the cost of discipleship—you needed to love Him more than family, friends or the things of the world. In fact, the world hated those who became disciples of Jesus (John 15:19). The Messiah placed the Holy Spirit inside everyone who had saving faith so they would at last have the power to walk with God (Hebrews 8:10-11; Matthew 3:11; Mark 1:8; Luke 3:16; John 1:33).

5. But the only way they could receive this salvation was to throw in their lot with a ragtag bunch of social outcasts, selling everything in exchange for the Pearl of Great Price.

Jesus had warned Nicodemus only those born of the Spirit could enter the kingdom of God (John 3:5). This is what evangelicals call being born again—when someone is born of the Holy Spirit. Peter identified the filling of the Holy Spirit with the salvation God brought that day.

Ten years later, he shared the Gospel with a group of Gentiles at the house of Cornelius. Once again, the people were "devout" (Acts 10:2), but this time they received the Holy Ghost *while* Peter preached the Gospel, so there was no doubt they were born again. Because of this, Peter did not hesitate to baptize them, even though they weren't Jews. A similar event occurred when Ananias baptized Paul *after* he was born again (Acts 9:17-18).

Being Added to the Church Meant a Total Change

Three thousand were added to the church. This meant they were baptized in water, continued in submission to the apostles' doctrine, met daily for Bible study and shared their meals and material wealth with other Christians waiting expectantly for Christ to return.

As H.D. McDonald said, "The people of the New Testament rejoiced in being redeemed, and were called upon to live redeemed lives. What was in Stoicism an unrealizable demand and an unattainable ideal was in apostolic preaching a vital experience. Of course the Christian Converts did not find in themselves any immediate abolishing of sin, but they did find such an expansion of the powers of life as made all things seem possible. As Weinel puts it, 'They *experienced* redemption.'"[1]

Scripture teaches baptism and Holy Spirit birth are complementary. "Not by works of righteousness which we have done, but according to his mercy he saved us, by the washing of regeneration, and renewing of the Holy Ghost" (Titus 3:5). As seen earlier, there were accounts of persons who were born again *before* they were water baptized. The Holy Spirit does not *necessarily* come into the believer when he is water baptized. (Most Bible scholars agree that Simon the magician believed and was baptized, but was not saved [Acts 8:13].) Of course, when water baptism is an external sign of saving faith, God gives His Spirit gladly. Nevertheless, God is not constrained for "*The wind blows where it wishes* and you hear the sound of it, but do not know where it comes from and where it is going; so is everyone who is born of the Spirit" (John 3:7-8 NASB).

If there were any among the 3,000 who were not born again,

the intensive counseling and follow-up in the womb of the church would have given them ample opportunity to get saved. In any case, they lived their lives according to the teachings of Jesus Christ and the apostles and obeyed God to the extent of their knowledge. This was what later Christians called the "means of grace." (see appendix C)

Being Saved from Sin unto Righteousness

Throughout Christian history, the context of salvation and religious life was an attempt to please God. If you were not saved from sin, you were not saved.

But today, many evangelists in America preach salvation primarily as being saved *from the consequences* of sin. Even a hundred years ago, a healthy moral culture still existed in America. This residual Judeo-Christian ethic was not only reflected in our laws and customs, it was also part of what it meant to be an American. Almost everyone agreed to the basic moral principles of the Ten Commandments. If someone "got religion," it meant they had to give up the worldly lifestyle. That was one reason so few got religion.

As American culture has declined morally, so has the understanding of foundational truths. The meanings of words have become twisted. Pursuit of happiness has now become pursuit of pleasure. Freedom *of* religion now means freedom *from* religion.

In the same way, the modern Gospel evolved from "If your right hand makes you stumble, cut it off and throw it from you; for it is better for you to lose one of the parts of your body, than for your whole body to go into hell (Matthew 5:30 NASB), to "I'm not perfect—just forgiven."

The 3,000 individuals who were added to the church on the day of Pentecost had almost no similarity to the typical American who goes forward in an altar call. The context of sin and judgment, law and righteousness, for the most part no longer exists.

No one would consider giving an altar call for a group of five-year-old children because they don't have sufficient knowledge of sin and repentance. But according to Ray Comfort, the typical American has so little understanding of God's law and the penalty for sin that repeating a salvation prayer may do more harm than good. Comfort learned the truth the hard way.

"Many years ago, before I understood the function of God's Law, I told a prostitute of God's love and was delighted that she immediately began weeping. Unbeknown to me, her tears were not tears of godly sorrow for sin, but merely an emotional response to the need of a father's love. In my ignorance, I joyfully led her in a sinner's prayer. However, I was disappointed sometime later when she fell away, and her tender heart became very callous toward the things of God."[2]

This book does not provide a rationale for doing away with altar calls. Rather, it shows with empirical data the modern altar call is deceptive if it implies that everyone who comes forward and repeats a formula "salvation prayer" is saved at that moment. Furthermore, without an after-meeting where seekers can pour out their souls—and hopefully repent—and get counseling and prayer from trained ministers, the percentage of true conversions is drastically reduced.

Lastly, trusting inquirers are automatically saved at the altar is as illogical as trusting in water baptism alone and is largely responsible for the current moral crisis in American evangelical churches.

The Hour Of Decision

Beth volunteered when her pastor asked for workers to serve as counselors at the Franklin Graham crusade. She was already an experienced worker, having helped lead many to the Lord. She didn't think this would be any different than witnessing to family, friends and neighbors. She was shown a video on how to deal with people who made a decision for Christ at the altar. She was given a counseling booklet that explained "How to be sure that Christ has forgiven my sin," and, for the person who didn't understand why they had said the salvation prayer, "How to know what I've done."

Beth was bothered that the crusade staff assumed everyone who came forward was ready to pray a salvation prayer. With all her witnessing in the past, it took many long hours of counseling before people were willing to truly commit their lives to God. And the people she spent the most time with, many who claimed to have made a decision for Christ, exhibited no evidence of a new life.

Because of this, she was careful never to lead someone to the conclusion they were saved unless they bore obvious fruit (Galatians 5:22-25). To be honest, the ones who constantly wanted to be assured of their salvation were the very ones she considered to be deceived.

On the first and second nights of the crusade, she helped move tracts and books to the tables and didn't pay attention to the altar call. The first night she helped three people fill out the "My Commitment" tract and the second night she helped two. She wondered whether she should disobey her superior and spend all her time with just one person. Most of the people she counseled seemed confused or distracted. (Of course, the noise and movement all around her added to the confusion.) Because she didn't have enough time to determine their true condition, all she could do was pray for the best and resolve to contact them the next day at their homes.

On the last night of the crusade, Beth heard Franklin Graham lead a large group of people who had come forward in the usual salvation prayer: "Dear Lord Jesus, I am a sinner. I need your forgiveness. I am sorry for my sins. I believe that you died for me. I want to turn from my sinful life. I now invite you to come into my heart.

I want to trust you as my savior. I want to follow you as my Lord. Amen."[1]

Beth hoped that many in the group were led of the Holy Spirit when they prayed ... that many were given the gift of repentance ... that God had saved them. But Franklin went on: "If you prayed that prayer and meant it, God has just forgiven you. He has just cancelled the debt. He just washed the slate clean. ... He's dumped your file. ... He cannot even recall it, even if He wants. The debt's cancelled and right now at 4:39 on 17 March, this is your spiritual birthday. This is the day that you've been born again ... you will never stand in front of God for judgment of sin."[2]

She stood still, frozen with horror. She knew from personal experience most of the people who said the prayer were not saved at that moment. Every fiber of her being wanted to cry out, "Don't tell them that!" But it was too late. "Don't they see? Don't they know what they've done? No wonder there are so many confused people. He just told people that they'd never stand before the judgment seat of God!"

It was then she remembered the follow-up system. She thanked God BGEA insisted counselors call inquirers within forty-eight hours of the crusade, church ministers visit the homes and each inquirer enroll in a Bible study course, giving them every opportunity to be saved.

Beth is an imaginary character, but she expresses the sentiment of ministers like Ray Comfort who know the problems of modern evangelism firsthand. Some evangelism programs systematically lead unrepentant sinners in a salvation prayer and then spend precious counseling time assuring them they made the right decision.[3]

How different this modern attitude is from the understanding of D.L. Moody in the late 1800s. His after-meeting workers were not trained to convince seekers they were saved. Rather, he taught his counselors how to help inquirers see their lost condition and lead them to repentance. Here's a sample of his "How to Deal with Inquirers" training:

"Those who want Christ are divided into four classes; --First professing Christians; second, those who think others are worse than they; third, the backsliders, and fourth, those who are completely broken down in sin." After dealing with the different needs of the four classes of inquirers, Moody concluded, "What I want to impress upon you is that, to bring men to Christ, all that is necessary is to know, feel, understand and be able to explain the Word of God."[4]

While Moody saw it necessary for altar workers to "know, feel, understand and explain the Word of God," today's altar workers are encouraged, in some cases, to spend no more than fifteen minutes with each inquirer.[5]

Moody "urged upon his 'personal workers,' as he called them, 'patient and thorough dealing with each case, no hurrying from one to another. Wait patiently, and ply them with God's word, and think, oh! think what it is to win a soul for Christ, and don't grudge the time spent on one person."[6]

Moody never led anyone in a salvation prayer and never did anything that might interrupt the convicting work of the Holy Spirit. He once said, "I doubt a man's conversion who has not joy. If a man who thought he was converted last night told me he had not joy I should not believe in his thorough conviction."[7]

Contrast that with today's push to convince inquirers they are born again. John MacArthur reported, in some evangelism training seminars he attended, the counselors "were taught to tell 'converts' that any doubt about their salvation is satanic and should be dismissed."[8]

MacArthur takes grave exception to this practice, saying, "Scripture encourages us to examine ourselves to determine if we are in the faith (2 Corinthians. 13:15). Peter wrote, 'Be all the more diligent to make certain about his calling and choosing you' (2 Peter 1:10). It is right to examine our lives and evaluate the fruit we bear, for 'each tree is known by its own fruit' (Luke 6:44)."[9]

Edwards, Whitefield and Wesley

Before the twentieth century, evangelicals (Calvinist and Arminian) taught conversion as a definite, mystical event, orchestrated by a sovereign God. The pre-twentieth century understanding of salvation lined up with the Bible. "Therefore if any man be in Christ, he is a new creature: old things are passed away; behold, all things are become new" (2 Corinthians 5:17).

Both George Whitefield and John Wesley taught the born-again experience as definite, complete and identifiable.[1] If someone asked a new convert about his experience, he could describe exactly how he had changed. How different that is from today, when pastors have to twist the arms of kids for testimonies of how they "got saved" at church camp.

Before the twentieth century, salvations were rare, but real. As Whitefield taught it, the new creation was not a "mere metaphor." "It was as self-evident and palpable as a 'tasteless palate' suddenly brought alive at a sumptuous feast."[2] People received the illumination of the Holy Spirit ... not just the convincing message of a talented evangelist.

Charles Spurgeon summed up the sentiment: "I do not come into this pulpit hoping that perhaps somebody will of his own free will return to Christ. My hope lies in another quarter. I hope that my Master will lay hold of some of them and say, 'You are mine, and you shall be mine. I claim you for myself.' My hope arises from the freeness of grace, and not from the freedom of the will."[3]

From Church Membership to Personal Experience

Before Whitefield and Wesley, large, impersonal gatherings were rare. Local ministers were responsible for "making disciples," and the idea of people "getting saved" outside the context of a local body was unusual. Reformation Protestants believed in infant baptism, adult confirmation and church membership. All the needs of the saints were met in the sacraments. Salvation could not be separated from the ordinances of the local body. If a person wanted to "get saved," he or she could become a local church member.

When George Whitefield and John Wesley came on the scene, they preached a personal salvation not controlled by church membership. They burned with the fire of revival, calling for repentance and holiness. Their standard for salvation was a born-again experience. Anything less was worse than no religion at all because false religion obscures the true condition of the soul. Consequently, they were denied access to the pulpits of most churches.

This set evangelical Christianity on a course which de-emphasized salvation through sacraments, ordinances and church membership and created a new approach to evangelism. (Of course, this wasn't really a new approach at all. Personal salvation is just as much a New Testament teaching as submission to elders.) Luther and Calvin had both declared personal salvation as necessary, but they did it in the context of the local church. Luther's born-again experience was just as definite and complete as Whitefield's and Wesley's.[4]

The new evangelism emphasized the born-again experience as a definite conversion, identifiable at a specific time, accompanied by feelings. Whitefield explained: "Every one who has but the least concern for the salvation of his precious, his immortal soul, having such promises, such an hope, such an eternity of happiness set before him, should never cease watching, praying, and striving till he find a *real inward, saving change wrought in his heart, and thereby knows of the truth that he dwells in Christ and Christ dwell in him*."[5] (my italics)

The Calvinist-Arminian differences didn't influence the methods of the popular evangelists. Whitefield encouraged seekers to give their lives to God almost as fervently as Wesley did. Wesley also believed God was sovereign in conversions.

All evangelists call people out of their complacency. They tell people they will die in their sins unless they are converted. Whether the conversion takes place before or after the call for repentance is not the issue. The most important thing is that the evangelist explains the new birth process in a way that is clear to seeker and saved alike.

Large Crowds, Large Problems

As evangelism moved from the pulpit to the open field, preaching to unknown crowds presented new problems. There was no congregational peer-pressure to prevent emotional outbursts. Crowds were a mixture of churched and unchurched from all levels of society, so anything could happen, including physical and verbal disturbances. Wesley ignored the outbursts, thinking it wiser than calling attention to them. Whitefield seemed to encourage displays of emotion. "Outcries and repentant groans soon punctuated every sermon. The traditional Sunday sermon seemed boring by comparison. While he was in the town, hysteria often prevailed. The next morning he was gone and the local minister had to deal with the aftermath."[6]

Jonathan Edwards disliked many of the negative effects of Whitefield's evangelism. He, like so many pastors of the day, had to deal with the real problems after emotions died down. But all pre-twentieth century evangelicals agreed on two things: Salvation was definite and complete,[7] and persons who exhibited no lasting change were never saved to begin with. They were "false appearances, corrupt mixtures, even counterfeits."[8]

Salvation was Definite and Complete

Before the twentieth century, churches that taught the doctrine of "eternal security" included the necessary caveat that if someone didn't act saved, they probably never were. Over and over again we find in the writings of the most strident hyper-Calvinists emphatic resentment that anyone would suggest grace could result in sinful living. Of course, these great men of God were merely repeating the Gospel message ... echoing what Jesus, Paul and Peter said about the new birth so many times before.

"What shall we say then? Shall we continue in sin, that grace may abound? God forbid. How shall we, that are dead to sin, live any longer therein? ... even so we also should walk in newness of life" (Romans 6:1-4).

Although pre-twentieth century Arminianism allowed for a "falling away," it taught the more likely reason a church member would return to a sinful lifestyle was they were never born again. In either case, both sides taught the biblical truth that salvation was definite and complete and were quick to judge false conversions. Whitefield compelled his listeners to understand salvation as *nothing less than "a thorough, real, inward change of heart."*[9]

God Prepares People for Salvation

It was common understanding that the Holy Spirit prepared people before they could be born again. Jonathan Edwards identified no less than eight stages of salvation.

Erroll Hulse explains:

"[1] The first step in the conversion process was an awakening to danger, a sense of horror at being eternally lost. The natural state of a soul in sin is one of extreme wretchedness and misery.

[2] The second step was a response by the awakened soul to its appalling state. There was a measure of reformation in the person awakened, seeking to avoid sins which could exacerbate that condition of guilt and lostness. Also there was a looking for a solution and willingness to use the means of grace. (see Appendix C)

[3] The next move, the third, was a conviction of absolute dependence on God's sovereign power and grace. The source of help became clear. One would think that immediate refuge in God would be resorted to at this stage, but it was not always so. Recourse by the awakened was to their own strength and ability to find God. In this exercise they did not find the peace they were seeking.

[4] In the fruitlessness of their own endeavors a new conviction overcame them, namely, that God was just in their condemnation. He did not have to save them. He was not obliged to do so. Their own performances were futile. This was the fourth stage and it prepared the way for the dawning for the first time of the glory of God.

[5] The awakened soul began 'to see feelingly' or to be moved by the beauty of God. To Edwards this fifth stage was absolutely crucial. To him gracious religious affections were bedded in a person

having a truly inward love for the moral excellence and glorious attributes of God. It is not enough for sinners to see God as the source and centre of their own need, as if His existence were merely to meet their desires and satisfy their convenience. Reality is to see and appreciate the Godhood of God.

"All these five steps Edwards esteemed as 'preparatory to grace.' Again it is imperative to stress that these five steps were not a human work pushed forward and organized by the sinner and aided by his pastor as counselor. All preparatory work is by the Spirit.

[6] The next stage, the sixth, 'is an earnest longing of the soul after God and Christ.' This desire is the very opposite of that of the natural man, who is at enmity with God. It is one thing to recognize God's glory; it is another to desire Him.

[7] The seventh stage was one in which the awakened soul reposed in Christ and became aware of being delighted in Christ.

[8] The eighth step was assurance. Edwards regarded assurance as vital. A lack of assurance could hinder spiritual growth. Assurance that did not result in obedience and Christian practice was not genuine."[9]

The ministry of Jonathan Edwards was an essential part of the first Great Awakening. He worked with the Holy Spirit in preparing sinners for salvation. "Edwards taught that great affections, effects on the body, fluency and fervor of speech or of expression, zeal and confidence, together with moving testimonies—all these can fall short of the new birth."[11] For this and other reasons, he never encouraged sinners to do anything that might stop them short of absolute submission to God. (see appendices D,E and F)

Charles Finney

The theology and methods of Edwards, Whitefield and Wesley prepared the way for new innovations. In 1792, William Carey, the father of modern missions, published *An Enquiry into the Obligations of Christians to Use Means for the Conversion of Heathens.* The view that ministers should employ all the means at their disposal increasingly characterized nineteenth century Protestantism.[1]

Many saw this trend as a threat to the biblical truth of the sovereignty of God. In fact, when Carey proposed the formation of a missionary society to the president of a Baptist conference, he was dismissed with the opinion that if it pleased God to convert the heathen, God would do it without Carey's help.[2]

Many new means or methods were identified with Charles Finney, the father of modern evangelism: the mourner's bench (also called the anxious bench, altar, or penitent form), where seekers were asked to sit or kneel; the raising of hands or standing up in the congregation for those who wanted prayer; kneeling at seats; coming forward and giving the hand to the minister as a sign of need; and perhaps the most enduring of methods, the use of the "inquiry room," where penitents could receive counsel and prayer during what came to be called the after-meeting.[3]

The new methods were designed to persuade anxious sinners to immediately confront their lost condition. Charles Finney believed the Holy Spirit illuminated every man (John 1:9) and used the methods to inspire a commensurate response from sinners. The methods stimulated emotional excitement, once thought to be a hindrance to spiritual ministry.

Finney responded to the critics: "Because evils sometimes arise out of excited awakenings, they conclude we should dispense with excitement altogether. This can't be. There is indeed danger of abuses. In cases of great spiritual awakenings (as with all excitements), unintended evils may be expected. But that isn't any reason to give up excitement, for the best things are always liable to abuses."[4]

In retrospect, the only question we need to ask is whether Finney was assisting God's process or assuming too much. Many thought he had gone too far, like Moses striking the rock twice (Numbers 20:1). In addition, many critics were skeptical of the results.[5]

To those who pointed out *any* conversions were invaluable, no matter how obtained, one critic said, "If truth and righteousness are made to suffer for the purpose, more is lost than won by the result. We must not do wrong, even to gain a soul for heaven. And if for one thus gained, ten should be virtually destroyed, by the very process employed to reach the point, who will say that such a method of promoting Christianity would be deserved to be approved?"[6]

The Altar Call

Finney is credited with starting the altar call. But, to be accurate, many evangelists before Finney asked penitents to come forward. In 1799, Baptists, Methodists and Presbyterian ministers combined efforts in the first camp meetings and used an "altar" or "mourner's bench."

Finney popularized methods that were later adopted by lesser men who used them without the necessary safeguard of competent counseling. Gradually, evangelists depended more on the methods to gain converts. A contemporary critic commented on this new type of minister: "There may be no power whatever in his ordinary walk or conversation, to enforce the claims of religion. … The truth is, he has no capacity, no inward sufficiency, for the ordinary processes of evangelical labor. Much is required to be a faithful minister of the New Testament; whilst small resources in comparison are needed for that semblance of power, to which a man may attain by the successful use of the system now in view."[7]

The Ordinary Processes of Evangelism

In the 1800s, the making of converts was hard work, often taking days, weeks or even months until God deigned to save them. Ministers used counseling in concert with the Holy Spirit to unravel the tangled web of lies that prevented sinners from repenting and giving all to God. ("The heart is ... desperately wicked, who can know it?" [Jeremiah 17:9].) Ministers served as pre-marriage counselors rather than Las Vegas chaplains. If a counselor was patient and waited on the Holy Spirit, sinners only needed to be saved once.

Perhaps the most famous counselor was Ichabod Spencer, the "Bunyan of Brooklyn." In the 1800s, he recorded 20,000 counseling sessions over twenty-two years. The following is an excerpt of perhaps his most difficult case:

"She became interested on the subject of religion, and attended the meeting for religious inquiry week after week. ... She appeared to understand and believe all that was said to her. Her convictions of sins seemed to be clear and deep. ... I exercised all my skill to ascertain her hindrances, to show her the state she was in, and lead her to Christ. It was all in vain ...

Her condition distressed me. I had said everything to her that I could think of which I supposed adapted to her state of mind. I had referred her to numerous passages in the Bible ... and yet she said she was as far from the kingdom of heaven as ever, her heart was unmoved, and at enmity against God.

Just at this period I accidentally met her one morning in the street ... Offering her my hand, I asked, 'Sarah, have you given your heart to God?'

'No sir,' said she, tremulously.

'Don't you think you ought to?'

"I know I ought to."

'Don't you think you ought to do it to-day?'

'Yes, I do.'

'Then will you?'

'Yes, I will,' said she, emphatically.

'Good-bye,' said I, and instantly left her.

A day or two afterwards I saw her. ... she wanted to tell me how she felt and how she had been affected. She said that ... her mind was at rest—that she now loved God. ... She united with the Church, and yet honors her profession.

"This is the only case in which I have ever led any person to make such a promise. I doubt the propriety of doing it. (my italics) I did not really intend it in this instance. ... The resolutions of an unconverted sinner are one thing, and the operations of the Holy Spirit are quite another. They may coincide, indeed, and if such resolutions are made in the spirit of a humble reliance of God, they may be beneficial. ... But if such resolutions are made in self-reliance, they are rash, and will seldom be redeemed. ... If anyone thinks that he has turned to God without the special aids of the Holy Spirit, it is probable that he has never turned to God at all."[8]

Please note: Spencer never again asked a sinner to make such a promise, and in 20,000 counseling sessions, it never occurred to him that it might be beneficial to lead someone in a salvation prayer. Spencer was typical of evangelical ministers before Billy Sunday changed the salvation template.

The New Processes of Evangelism

Finney was not responsible for the abuses of those who followed, but the die was cast. All the clichés and quackery epitomized by Sinclair Lewis's Elmer Gantry began with the use of the altar call. Finney's methods in the hands of incompetents and charlatans would ultimately produce millions of spurious conversions. The methods became the easiest way for ungifted and lazy men to produce "converts" with little effort.

Proponents of the new measures said they were "shaking up" the dry formalism of the past. But perhaps in the end, all new measures become old, and that which was unique soon becomes common. One contemporary critic made this point: "They propose to rouse the Church from its dead formalism. And to do this effectively, they strike off from the old ways of worship, and bring in new and strange practices, that are adapted to excite attention. These naturally produce a theatrical effect, and this is taken at once for an evidence of waking life in the congregation. One measure, losing its power in proportion as it becomes familiar, leads to the introduction of another."[9]

The nineteenth century altar call never implied people who came forward would be immediately saved. It merely invited sinners to come to an after-meeting where trained counselors would answer questions and help seekers in the process of repentance. But all this was about to change.

As the altar call became more common, the numbers that came forward increased. This created a need for more counselors in the after-meeting and encouraged a streamlining of the process of counseling and follow-up. Through the changing of generations, the biblical understanding of the sovereignty of God was slowly replaced by a modern psychological perspective. The definition of saving faith evolved slowly from a supernatural gift given by God into a decision of the will.

Early reports in the 1800s suggested a very small percentage of the people who went forward in altar calls were "hopefully saved." As the decades passed, the percentages grew. But throughout the 1800s, a 10 percent salvation rate among those who came to the altar was considered spectacular. Then Billy Sunday changed everything.

Billy Sunday Changes Everything

Billy Sunday was a successful professional baseball player when God saved him at the Pacific Garden Mission in Chicago in 1886. The altar call invited him to come forward to confess his sins, seek Christ's forgiveness and live in obedience to Christ's teachings. His born-again salvation experience was definite and complete. He soon started preaching at the YMCA and other places, where he would ask penitents to come to the after-meetings for prayer and individual counsel.

Within a short time, Sunday was hired by the popular evangelist J. Wilber Chapman to serve as an advance man and sometimes preacher. Chapman, like his mentor, D.L. Moody, had very high standards. He taught Sunday the ropes, always emphasizing the effective use of the after-meeting and inquiry room. But when Sunday started his own organization in 1896, he dropped the inquiry room entirely and changed the "Decision Card" (used to get penitent information for follow-up) to a "Convert's Pledge Card." He started calling everyone who came forward a convert and used his own celebrity status to lure them to the front.

"How many of you will settle the great question without the delay of another minute, by coming forward to take me by the hand, and by doing so confess and accept Jesus Christ as your personal Savior? Will you come?"[1]

Setting up the false premise that a physical act was the same as saving faith, Sunday encouraged the lie of a 100 percent conversion rate to be reported in the press: "CONVERTS RUSHED TO GRASP HANDS OF BILLY SUNDAY ... publicly acknowledging their belief in Jesus Christ as their savior, and expressing their repentance for sin, 425 men, women and children of all ages and types, surged down the sawdust trail to the platform at the tabernacle last night to grasp the hand of Billy Sunday and to be enrolled as professing Christians."[2]

Sunday coaxed various groups to come forward for absurd reasons, little of which had to do with the conviction of the Holy Spirit. He boasted that he "never gave an invitation where no one had come." [3]

"'Come on, you Masons,' or 'come on, sailors' or 'come on there, Wanamaker Store, you're a fine looking bunch.' At one time Sunday had worked on the railroad and was particularly eager to appeal to railroad men: If railroad workers were present, he sometimes shouted 'come on, Erie' or 'Boston and Maine' and wave a green lantern. At other times when other groups were present he would appeal to them by name, 'come on, Boston, come on people. Come on Roxbury. Come on Somerville. Come on, Newton. Don't, I beg you in the name of the Lord, refuse.' When young people's church groups were present, he invited them with a challenge: 'Come on, Epworth Leaguers, Christian Endeavors, everybody. What'll you do? What'll you do?' Sometimes he stood on top of the pulpit waving two American flags or a large church flag in order to stimulate the trail hitting. On 'Scotch Night' in Boston he called to the large Scotch delegation which had come with bagpipes and kilts, 'Come on Scotchmen. Show some of the grit of Wallace and Bruce.' And he waved a Scottish flag from his perch on the pulpit. To a Swedish delegation one night he shouted, 'Come on Swedes. The Swedes have never been cowards yet. So come on.'"[4]

Homer Rodeheaver, his music director of seventeen years, after pointing out the dishonesty of the practice, quit. "When he makes his proposition for everyone to come it loses its effect because people cannot see any definite, specific thing for which they should come."[5]

All the dire predictions made in the 1800s about the confusion and spurious conversions that could result from Charles Finney's new methods were fully realized with Sunday. Despite the warnings of contemporary pastors, Sunday never repented of his theatrics. Some pastors, seeing the abuse, abandoned Sunday's meetings, but most went along for the ride. Sunday left a trail of damage that later evangelists would have to repair.

With the intense competition of consumerism, ministers were tempted to take grievous shortcuts to assure higher numbers of converts. This temptation had always been present for every minister of the Gospel, but in the early twentieth century, "salvations" became as cheap and easy to obtain as the mass-produced goods pouring from the factories.

Decades before, D.L. Moody had also attracted large, excited crowds. But instead of encouraging emotional outbursts, he did everything he could to prevent them. One time in Glasgow, Scotland, the emotional pitch was so high, as a Christian magazine reported, the crowd "blocked the streets for hours and the excitement penetrated the meeting to such an extent that an inquiry meeting was not even attempted ... other revival movements seemed to have flourished on excitement, but this is at once killed by it; and instead of taking advantage of heated occasions, Mr. Moody waits for the night of quiet power and the whisper of the still small voice."[6]

Charles Goss wrote, "From the first moment to the last, the fact that he meant business, and not fireworks, oratory or theatricals was apparent."[7] For Moody, the sermon was the prelude to the after-meeting, where he threw himself into the fray of seekers. He counseled, prayed for and instructed the illuminated and confused alike, but never called someone a convert by virtue of an external act.

What is a Convert?

It is remotely possible Sunday considered all "seekers" to be "converts." Historically, a converted person is "a Christian ... a person who 'has religion,' who has experienced regeneration."[8] But because some Protestants believe an individual can experience conversion before God regenerates, it is possible Sunday considered a convert to be anyone who wanted to be a Christian and was willing to come forward. This is unlikely however, since Sunday changed the after-meeting counseling to instruction for Christians, indicating the presumption that everyone who came forward did so because he was saved.

The net result of calling everyone who came forward a "convert" forced some ministers to distance themselves from this modern innovation and caused a redefining of who was and wasn't born again. Since the term "convert" now meant "anyone who wants to be a Christian and is willing to go forward," Oswald Chambers (a contemporary of Sunday, best known for the book, *My Utmost for His Highest*) had to make a distinction:

"When a man fails in personal Christian experience, it is nearly always that he has never really *received* anything. The only sign that a man is saved is that he has received something from Jesus Christ. Our part as workers for God is to open men's eyes that they may turn themselves from darkness to light; but that is not salvation, that is conversion–the effort of a roused human being. I do not think it is too sweeping to say that the majority of nominal Christians are of this order; their eyes are opened, but they have received nothing. Conversion is not regeneration. This is one of the neglected factors in our preaching to day. When a man is born again, he knows it is because he has received something as a gift from almighty God and not because of his own decision. People register their vows, and sign their pledges, and determine to go through, but none of this is salvation."[9]

This definition of conversion fits exactly millions of Christians who have made hopeful decisions for Christ, but are not saved. Although it is alien to the historic and biblical definition of conversion, it is helpful to understand why most evangelical Christians are not born again.

Presumption that Everyone is Born Again

Sunday had forever changed the understanding of the altar call. From this point on, everyone who came forward was automatically considered a convert, and every evangelist, if he wanted to be considered a success, had to adopt this deception. No longer was it necessary to wait on God. Since everyone who came forward in an altar call was a convert, it allowed the after-meeting to be used for the efficient processing of new Christians. There were many practical advantages to ignoring the fact that most of the people who came forward were not born again.

First, since Sunday invited everyone to the front to shake his hand as a sign of conversion, there were simply too many converts to counsel in the traditional way. Second, since the *Convert's Pledge* card gave follow-up information to participating churches, if there were any spurious conversions, they could be sorted out later. Third, modern psychology taught that it was better to tell someone they were saved than to leave any doubt in their minds. Fourth, modern methods required definite standards and practices. The old inquiry room method of counseling and waiting on God taught by Moody and other evangelists since Finney was considered frustrating and inefficient ... like natural childbirth.

While Finney encouraged the birth process, Sunday ignored it. Finney taught his altar workers to recognize dilation, contractions and internal movements. The pre-Sunday counselor tried to serve as a midwife in concert with The Great Obstetrician, helping with, but never forcing a birth.

One of these was G. Campbell Morgan, a contemporary of Sunday. In 1905 he described the effective use of the after-meeting and inquiry room before Sunday changed the understanding of the altar call: "A word about the after-meeting ... I would rather have a dozen people constrained, convicted, and converted, than a hundred caught in some emotional movement, in which movement there is no real depth of conviction and result. ... The inquiry room is simply for inquiring souls to come that they may be intelligently dealt with about the spiritual perplexities. And that makes necessary the training of inquiry room workers. You cannot deal intelligently and correctly with a hundred at once.

Every case has an individual problem, and there are two words that cover the ground of such work, and these are the words diagnosis and direction. ... we have no business to tell any man he is saved. There's a point where we have to stand aside and let God and the man deal alone with each other. We can help, lead, point, counsel, warn, plead, but at last regeneration is the coming of God to the soul that comes to Him, and we have to draw aside and leave the individual to God."[10]

Contrast that with the description of an after-meeting at a Sunday crusade, where everyone who came forward was saved as long as they were willing to fill out a *Convert's Pledge* card.

"'I accept Jesus as my personal Savior.' This pledge is signed by every person who 'hits the sawdust trail' at the Sunday tabernacle. The cards are distributed ... pencils are passed out and the names, addresses, church affiliations or preferences of each person taken. ... The cards are distributed and signed after Sunday issues his final plea for converts and while the choir is still singing gospel songs. After the cards are signed they are collected by the secretaries, sorted according to church preference and address and handed over to the pastors of the various churches."[11]

Although 100 percent conversion was reported, the actual results were no better than those of D.L. Moody in the previous century.

Everyone knew a Billy Sunday convert was suspect. In fact, this perception was so widespread that "Sunday Convert" was a common term of derision. Torrey Johnson, founder of Youth for Christ, was kidded by a classmate at Wheaton College with the insult, "Got religion, have you? I suppose it's the Billy Sunday type. It'll last about six months."[12] William T. Ellis, a sympathetic biographer, in 1936 placed the percentage of true conversions at less than 10 percent of those who made decisions for Christ.[13]

Lyle W. Dorsett, a modern Sunday biographer, perhaps unwittingly gave a more accurate appraisal while trying to put the best possible light on Sunday's "box scores."

"If as little as five percent of the people who streamed forward between 1908 and 1920 were truly transformed, then Billy Sunday was reaching more people than any other preacher in America."[14]

D.L. Moody's church was not so blasé about the deceptive claims. When they did a follow-up on the cards given to them after a 1918 Chicago crusade, they found just 3 percent of the trail hitters thought they were saved at the altar.[15]

Sunday used every psychological trick in the book to increase the box scores. Some contemporary evangelists and pastors complained bitterly of his questionable practices and results, but that didn't stop many from adopting the new standard. After all, how could they compete with a traditional 5 percent salvation rate when *everyone* who came to Sunday's altar was converted? Never again would there be a famous evangelist like D.L. Moody who would spend hours with penitents to help determine their true condition.

Convert's Pledge becomes Salvation Prayer

There is little doubt Sunday's *Convert's Pledge* was the precursor to the present day salvation prayer. When he worked for J. Wilbur Chapman, he used a decision card that read: "I have an honest desire henceforth to live a Christian life. I am willing to follow any light God may give me. I ask the people of God to pray for me."[16]

Notice the penitent's decision to live for God never implied God had granted salvation. It followed the pre-Billy Sunday inquiry room practice of requesting prayer and dedicating oneself to God as a step *before* salvation. When Sunday changed it to a *Convert's Pledge* card, it became a public declaration of faith, later understood as a moment of conversion, similar to the understanding of today's salvation prayer.

It's easy to imagine how the *Pledge* evolved into a prayer simply by changing the way it was used. By the 1930s, pledge cards were called decision cards and included the basic content of today's salvation prayer. But still they were not spoken aloud.[17] There remained the Protestant sole fide reservation of making a verbal pronouncement that might be confused with a sacramental act. It wasn't until the 1950s that Billy Graham had his altar workers use the pledge as a repeat-after-me prayer, and later led large groups himself in the prayer *before* any counseling, completing the evolution to its present form.

Billy Sunday Evangelism Evolves

Billy Sunday was responsible for an unprecedented paradigm shift in evangelism practices and theology. The template for salvation had changed forever. It isn't stating it too strongly that evangelism can be identified as pre-Billy Sunday and post-Billy Sunday. As the pre-Billy Sunday ministers died off, so did the understanding of the workings of the Holy Spirit in the penitent.

Why did the evangelical community allow the big lie of 100 percent conversion to be perpetuated? There were many factors. Since the middle of the nineteenth century, a war for the soul of America was raging that threatened the very survival of what we now call Fundamental Christianity. Liberal theology from Germany and modern science openly challenged the authority of the Scriptures. Many denominations were in the process of adapting their theology to the new lights.

Billy Sunday was the champion of Fundamentalism. The old axiom, "The enemy of my enemy is my friend," certainly applied to Sunday. Several of D.L. Moody's successors were disgusted with Sunday's influence over evangelism, but veiled their criticism. In the end, perhaps they allowed the lie because it made evangelism look more powerful than ever before, able to compete with the lures of the modern world.

Survival Of The Fittest

In the beginning of the twentieth century, American society was gripped by economic, moral, cultural, scientific and religious shifts. As thousands of country folk moved to the city for high-paying factory jobs, competition caused instability in every aspect of life. Idolatry of success and status infected every level of society as truth was twisted to help sell products of every description.

Money had always been a primary force of change and with surplus goods pouring from the factories, advertising was increasingly used to create new appetites in the lower classes. Douglas W.

Frank identified advertising, salesmanship and a change in the public perception of truth as destabilizing factors in the psyche of the common man.

"The two or three decades after 1890 might well be called, as they were by a 1915 observer, 'the Age of Advertising.' ... No longer was its purpose simply to provide objective information about the location and price of particular items consumers were looking for; rather, its purpose was now to persuade those who had perceived no previous need for a product that they did indeed need and want a product."[1]

Sunday used every psychological tool to get people to come to the front and shake his hand. He transferred his understanding of the crowd from the baseball stadium to his present work. When his organization could afford it, he hired professional men to handle every aspect of promotion. Sunday told sponsoring pastors, "You can't conduct business as you did twenty-five years ago, neither can you religion. This is a day of specialists."[2]

"They arranged businessmen lunches and fund-raising dinners; they generated public interest by getting constant coverage in the local press; they arranged for Sunday's triumphal entry into the city: bands, speeches by dignitaries, and parades. By the opening hymn of the first meeting, the city was gripped by such a feverish excitement that the success of the revival was virtually assured."[3]

Contemporary evangelist R.A. Torrey commented, "Many of the evangelists are being ruined. ... A good deal of commercialism has been creeping into our work ... and I fear less dependence on God."[4]

Gospel of Morality

Sunday was the most political evangelist in American history. He appealed to the working man and ruling class alike. He attacked "city slicker" decadence with religious zeal, becoming the champion of decency, morality and family. Often he identified coming down the sawdust trail with patriotism.

"How many of you will pledge and promise and say, 'God,

I will stand by you and I'll stand by your cross, and I'll stand by the religion of Jesus Christ. I'll stand by the flag, I'll stand by my country—here I am, Lord'?"[5]

"Oh, do you want to know why you are not a Christian? You aren't man enough to be a Christian! You haven't manhood enough to get up and walk down the aisle and take me by the hand and say, 'I give my heart to Christ.' You haven't manhood enough to take my hand and go this afternoon and say, 'I hit the trail this afternoon and I'm going to live for Christ ...'"[6]

It is indisputable that Billy Sunday got people to come down the aisle to shake his hand. The problem was the vast majority of them came for some reason other than saving faith. Billy Sunday felt he was fighting back liberalism and modernism and was in competition with the lures of the world. Because he had no formal religious training, he didn't see how he was changing evangelical Christianity into just another religion devoid of supernatural power.

The pre-Billy Sunday evangelist felt personally responsible for the birth process and assumed penitents were lost until they "broke through." The post-Billy Sunday evangelist assumed penitents were born again and left any problems to the churches. This modern innovation streamlined the salvation process to the point that Billy Sunday was able to boast he made converts for "two dollars a soul."[7] How different this new religion was from that "old time religion" practiced by most ministers before Sunday.

Please notice the *italicized* words in this worker's manual of the Salvation Army from 1881 (before Sunday changed everything).

1. What is the ordinary condition of Sinners when you meet with them?
PREOCCUPIED: that is--
I. Taken up with the things of the world--
II. Rebels against God, and--
III. Condemned to everlasting death.
2. What is your business with them?
I. To secure their attention.

II. To persuade them to submit to God, and then--

III. To accept pardon through the blood.

3. How do you go about accomplishing this?

By talking to them, publicly in the open air and indoors about their own sin, ingratitude, and death; about judgment, hell and heaven; the love of God, and the voluntary suffering and death Jesus Christ endured on their behalf; concerning their influence on others, and other similar topics.

4. What do you do then?

Go amongst them in the after-meetings, or wherever you can find them, and converse with them *personally*–press the truth home– if only a little moved, convict them further. Make them feel, have no pity on them until they are willing to give up all and submit to God.

5. But suppose they are not willing to YIELD, although feeling much and admitting all you say?

Oh, find out, if you can, what is the *hindrance* and press them to *give it up*. Show them that it is better to cut off the right hand than, having two hands, to go into hell, into the fire that shall never be quenched.

6. Well, supposing they are willing to give up and be saved, what then?

Bring them out to the penitent form [an altar] before the people, and so test them further, and pledge them publicly, and, when there, offer them mercy, and pray with and for them. [Not a salvation prayer, or even a convert's pledge ... just praying for illumination, the gift of repentance and that God would save them.]

7. *What if they do not obtain salvation, what then?*

There is still something in the way; or it may be, as it frequently is simply their unbelief; in which case, encourage and instruct, and help them. Give them texts and explanation, and illustrations, and songs; and, above all, a lot of sympathy. Make them pray aloud for themselves. Sing words having faith in them. Make them look at the blood, and trust the loving, dying Christ. Push them into the fountain.

8. If they don't get satisfaction, what must be done next?

Never tell them they are saved, if they don't think so. When a man gets saved, God will tell him about it; and then he will not need you to tell him so. But encourage him to go on seeking; urge him to go and deal with God alone, and come again. Get his address; have him visited. Go after him yourself.

9. What are you to do next, if he gets saved?

Give God all the glory, and get everyone in the place to help you do it.

10. And what will you do with your convert when you have got him?

Having made him a saint, now make him into a soldier. That is, let him or her--

I. Sign the pledge [this is only *after* conversion]

II. Testify at once to the blessing he has found.

III. Take his name and address for The Army.

IV. Have him at the open-air the next night, with a badge on.

V. Watch over and care for him as if he were your *own*, and as if you will have to give an account of him at the last day, *which you will most certainly have to do.*[8]

Sunday made no apologies for his impatience with the methods of the Salvation Army and the ministers who came before him.

"Some people think that they can't be converted unless they go down on their knees in the straw at a camp meeting, unless they pray all hours of the night and all days of the week while some old brother storms heaven in prayer. … What I want and preach is the fact that a man can be converted without any fuss."[9]

The inquiry room seemed a relic of the past, because as his wife boasted, "He made it (the question of salvation) so simple that there was no need for inquiry rooms."[10]

Unfortunately, most post-Sunday two dollar converts were incapable of acting like Christians. This forced concerned ministers like Dawson Trotman of the Navigators to demand extended follow-up to give converts an opportunity to get saved and ministers like Bill Bright of Campus Crusade for Christ to offer converts an opportunity to get saved a second time (he called it "sanctification") so they'd have the power to stop sinning.

The Navigators

Dawson Trotman taught his Navigators never to lead people in a decision for Christ unless they could be followed-up for at least twenty weeks, thus, giving them at least twenty weeks to get saved. How did he come to this point? Why did he break with other post-Billy Sunday evangelists that left the problem of spurious conversions in the hands of the churches? The following is his story:

Trotman made a typical decision for Christ at age fourteen when he joined the Presbyterian Church in Lomita, California in 1920. He exhibited no change in his sinful lifestyle and continued to lie and steal.

Later, at a Christian Endeavor meeting, a guest speaker illustrated God's offer of salvation by offering a gold watch to anyone who would accept it. Trotman jumped up and the speaker led him to a supposed second commitment to the Lord. He continued to lie and steal and started to smoke, get drunk and use profanity. Whenever he'd get in trouble, he'd call on God, but as soon as the storm passed, he'd return to his sinful ways. But in 1926, God saved him. Now, for the first time in his life, he had the workings of the Holy Spirit and was able by the power of God to overcome sin. He was born again, and the whole town knew it.

He started witnessing to anyone and everyone. According to one of his friends, he would pick up hitchhikers and "within two minutes he would be witnessing, and everyone he picked up accepted Christ in the car."[11] Trotman asked God to give him at least one soul a week. After a dry spell, he started a part-time job managing a miniature golf course. "This answered his prayer, for in order to bring in business he would invite a group of high schoolers in for a free game of starters. Afterward he presented the Gospel to them and easily got enough decisions to catch up on his quota. But though decisions increased, something did not seem right. Dawson withdrew his request for one soul a week until God should lead him to ask again. God never did."[12]

Trotman Compensates for Billy Sunday Theology

Trotman led countless people in decisions for Christ that meant little or nothing. Here he describes in his own words what caused him to see the rotten fruit of Sunday evangelism:

"One day, years ago, I was driving along in my little Model T Ford and saw a young man walking down the street. I stopped and picked him up. As he got into the car he swore. ... I reached in my pocket and said, Lad, read this.

"He looked up at me and said, 'Haven't I seen you somewhere before?'...We figured out that we had met the year before on the same road. ... He had accepted Jesus Christ as his savior. ... A year later there was no more evidence of the new birth and the new creature in this boy than if he had never heard of Jesus Christ."[13]

Trotman was convicted of the Holy Spirit that the boy's decision for Christ was ineffective. Within a short time, Trotman repented of having led so many into superficial commitments. "The hit-and-run evangelism he and others had practiced for years, resulting only in the 'survival of the fittest,' he now condemned as dead wrong."[14]

He realized decisions were useless without true conversion. He didn't state it that way, for he was a twentieth century evangelist, but no other interpretation explains his reluctance to lead people in a decision after his revelation. Trotman believed it was impossible for saved people to lose their salvation, so why was he reluctant to lead them in a decision for Christ, even knowing most would not "survive" (a euphemism for leading a victorious Christian life)? Isn't avoiding hell the main thing?

Trotman's Own Conversion

When Trotman was fourteen, he had made a decision for Christ that bore rotten fruit. When he was a senior in high school, he made another decision for Christ that bore rotten fruit. Both these decisions did nothing more than point out his need of a savior. After getting drunk on his graduation night, he wrote in his journal, "It's just not in me to do right. ... I'm a loser."[15]

But God enrolled Trotman in another school, where the knowledge of sin and holiness was taught by God's law, leading him to Christ (Galatians 3:24). After a six-year struggle of faith, God saved him. His first two professions of faith resulted in absolutely no ability to resist sin, and he had no evidence of the Holy Spirit within. But Billy Sunday theology prevented him from understanding these two decisions were merely mile-markers on the road of illumination, or as Billy Graham would say, a stage of gestation.[16]

After his ministry-changing road experience, Trotman started the Navigators specifically to prevent the destruction caused by easy decisions. He taught the Navigators, "You can lead a man to Christ in a couple of minutes to a couple of hours, but it takes twenty weeks to a couple of years to adequately follow him up."[17]

Bill Bright Compensates for Billy Sunday Theology

Bill Bright was, in several ways, the most effective evangelist of the twentieth century. Not since Charles Finney has one man's theology so completely influenced the spread of the Gospel. Like Finney in the nineteenth century, Bill Bright not only preached to thousands, but more importantly, for maximum growth, instructed countless saints how to witness effectively.

But after almost a half century of service to God, he realized the vast majority of the people who "got saved" through his ministry acted no differently than heathen. I remember the day in 1997 I heard him discuss on his radio program the idea that the "lifestyles of born-again Christians are virtually indistinguishable from those of nonbelievers."[18] He said essentially that the saying of a "salvation prayer" didn't assure a person would exhibit the Christian life.

I thought he was at a crossroad in his approach to evangelism. I put down the saw I was holding and steadied the sheet of plywood I was cutting so as to hear every syllable. I hoped he was about to confess remorse for his part in the scandal of modern evangelism. But unfortunately, he blamed this tragedy on a lack of sanctification in the church and assumed no responsibility for spurious conversions.

Instead of coming to the effective solution proposed by Dawson Trotman, and to a lesser extent, Billy Graham (don't lead someone in a decision unless you are willing to follow him up, thus giving illuminated sinners opportunity to get saved in God's time), Bright came up with a non-confrontational reason for someone to get saved a second time. He acknowledged most modern decisions had no power to change people, so he suggested they get "filled with the Holy Spirit." In order to do this, people needed to repent and yield control of their lives to Jesus Christ.

The reinstituting of repentance and giving Jesus Christ Lordship over one's life was a welcome step backward to the pre-twentieth century understanding of salvation. "Repent, and be baptized, every one of you, in the name of Jesus Christ for the remission of your sins" (Acts 2:38). This was a tacit acknowledgment that modern evangelism, by eliminating repentance and yielding control of one's life to God as a integral part of salvation, had stripped most decisions of any real meaning. But instead of saying most conversions were spurious, Bright suggested the evidence of salvation was only available if someone were filled with the Holy Spirit as a *second* act of grace he identified as "sanctification."

This enabled Bright to offer millions of carnal Christians a second chance to get saved, without telling them they were lost. This was similar to the Faustian bargain Billy Graham made when he emphasized follow-up without leveling with the thousands of people who came to the altar about the possibility they were only illuminated--or in a stage of gestation.

Bright was largely responsible for popularizing what A.W. Tozer (known best for his book, *Knowledge of the Holy*) called a "heresy" in the evangelical community in his book, *I Call It Heresy.*

"We are saved by accepting Christ as our savior; we are sanctified by accepting Christ as our Lord; we may do the first without the second. ... salvation apart from obedience is unknown in the sacred scriptures. ...What a tragedy that in our day we often hear the gospel appeal made on this kind of basis: 'Come to Jesus! You don't have to obey anyone. You do not have to change anything; You don't have to give up anything, alter anything, surrender anything, give back anything--just come to Him and believe in Him as Saviour!'"[19]

Tozer said the practical effect of this heresy was "probably less than one out of ten evangelicals knows anything experientially about the new birth."[20]

Blinded By the Bright

As a professional salesman, Bill Bright was proficient at presenting products in the best possible light. As an evangelist, he made it so easy to accept Jesus that 80,000 (80 percent of 100,000) Russians prayed the salvation prayer at one of his events. In 1988, in the country of Sudan alone, there were almost five million "decisions" for Christ (quotation marks by source).[21]

Bill Bright is typical of twentieth century evangelists who were ambivalent in their understanding of salvation. He recognized a definite crossing over when his father was saved. Bright said, "My father was a totally different man."[22] But his own decision for Christ seemed uneventful. In fact, one could argue it was only a stage of gestation (see Jonathan Edward's fourth step on page 37), for he wasn't aware of anything "dramatic or emotional," but became more aware of what a sinner he was.[23] His comment is similar to Luther's, Whitefield's and Wesley's pre-faith observations and has no similarity to the "all things have become new" descriptions of salvation in the Bible (2 Corinthians 5:17; John 3:3,5; Ephesians 2:10; 4:23; Colossians 3:10-11).

Bright's Campus Crusade for Christ is a multifaceted Christian ministry. His *Four Spiritual Laws* tract has been given to over four billion people and over five billion people have viewed his *Jesus* film. The Billy Graham Evangelistic Association and numerous other church and para church organizations have used his materials, making the theology of Bill Bright (from the perspective of population influenced) the single most influential version of the Gospel in history.

But was his Gospel based *entirely* on the Word of God or was it shaped more by his own salvation experience? Most great evangelists saw themselves as the worst of sinners when God saved them. Bright had a more modern view. While most great men of God struggle with repentance from dead works, Bright searched for purpose and meaning in life. Bright's salvation in 1945 was not so much an appeal for a clean conscience (1 Peter 3:21) as awareness that God could improve his prospects.

Bright elevated the biblical principle of prosperity and peace with God above the message of forgiveness of sin and avoidance of hell as the primary reason for accepting Christ as Savior.

Bright Dilutes Gospel because of a "Revelation"

Bright's first Gospel tract in 1958 followed a more traditional approach to salvation, beginning with man's sin and separation from God. But when it was revised a few years later, he changed it so it would appeal to more people. In his book, *Come Help Change the World*, he tells how it happened:

"I was in bed just at the point of going to sleep, when suddenly there came clear as a bell to my conscious mind the fact that there was something wrong about starting the *Four Laws* on the negative note of man's sinfulness. ... I felt that few people would say 'No' to Christ if they truly understood how much He loves them and how great is His concern for them. ... Some time later, one of the girls said to me, 'I was so distressed over your change in the presentation that I wept that night. I was afraid that you were beginning to dilute the gospel and that you were no longer faithful to the Lord, because you placed such a strong emphasis on the love of God rather than on man's sin. Now in retrospect, I realize of course that this is one of the greatest things that has ever happened to the Campus Crusade ministry'"[24]

Bright emphasized mankind needs a savior for the sake of a legal exchange, not because sinners without Christ can't keep the Law. If one accepted Jesus as the legal requirement demanded by God, he reasoned, the need for a struggle of faith was eliminated, and avoiding hell was a bonus.

Unfortunately, Bright ignored the biblical truth of the Law as schoolmaster and employed a modern psychological perspective, which ignored the need for true repentance in favor of a hopeful decision of the will. Like many modern theologians who interpret the Scriptures from a psychological perspective, Bright equated faith with hope and repentance with sorrow. This, coupled with an ignorance of the inexorable link between repentance and faith, has contributed to the greatest crisis in evangelical history.

Evidence of Salvation No Longer Necessary

While Finney taught conversion instantly changed the man,[25] Bright told people not to worry if they didn't know if they were truly saved. Gone was the evangelical understanding expressed in Jonathan Edwards words: "Nothing deserves the name religion that falls short of a remarkable change of disposition, created in the heart by the Holy Spirit, and showing itself in unselfish love for the things of God and in a burning desire for Christian conduct for all men."[26]

Bright acknowledged the workings of the Holy Spirit and a visible change in a person's behavior as *possible* signs of salvation, but said these indicators were not necessary and counseled anxious sinners not to trust their feelings but rather, the promise of God's Word.[27]

But hope is not faith (Hebrews 11:1), neither is believing a scripture applies to you. Hope and believing scripture may *precede* faith, or be a function of faith, but not necessarily.

Jonathan Edwards commented over 200 year ago on equating hope with faith:

"Those who aren't saved, think it disastrous to enter into self examination since their 'faith' is based solely on hope. If a person has nothing but hope to 'prove' he's saved, then to question that hope would undo his entire position. Those who insist on a person's living by faith, when they have no experience, and are in very bad frames, are very absurd in their notions of faith. What they mean by faith is, believing that they are in a good estate. Hence they count it a dreadful sin for them to doubt of their state, whatever frames they are in, and whatever wicked things they do, because it is the great and heinous sin of unbelief; and he is the best man, and puts most honor upon God, that maintains his hope of his good estate the most confidently and immovably, when he has the least light or experience. ... If this be faith, the Pharisees had faith in an eminent degree; some of whom Christ teaches, committed the unpardonable sin against the Holy Ghost"[28]

Believing the Gospel doesn't automatically make you a Christian any more than believing your house is on a firm foundation will automatically help your house withstand the wind. Jesus warned his disciples, "Therefore whosoever heareth these sayings of mine, *and doeth them*, I will liken him unto a wise man, which built his house upon a rock" (Matthew 7:24).

Did Bill Bright ever doubt the success of his theology and methods? He was quick to say, "Only the Lord knows who is making sincere commitments."[29] Nevertheless, he was sensitive to the criticism that many fell away because of inadequate follow-up. In 1971, he drafted a thirty-point rebuttal to those who found fault with his ministry. His last point sums up the sentiment of the document:

"The Holy Spirit is the only one that can adequately follow up and help the new convert to grow and mature in his faith. Encourage the new converts to grow and depend on the Holy Spirit and not on your clever ideas or on excellent follow-up material."[30]

In this respect, Bright differed significantly from Billy Graham, who considered follow-up to be absolutely essential.

Bright's argument that the Holy Spirit does the follow-up only makes sense if you assume the converts are truly saved and the Holy Spirit lives within them. Graham's follow-up worked regardless of whether or not the converts were saved.

The Billy Graham Formula
S+C+F=D(.25)=B

Sermon+Counseling+Follow-up=Decisions x 25%=Born-again experiences

Like Trotman and Bright, Billy Graham took measures to compensate for the fundamental flaw of Sunday evangelism. Even with the handicap of having to treat everyone who came forward as a convert, Graham fashioned a formula for success. His three-prong approach of excellent sermons, altar counseling and intensive follow-up by counselors and churches provided penitents with numerous opportunities to hear the Gospel and repent, resulting in, according to Graham, a possible 25 percent success rate.[1] Although this seems like an improvement over the 5 to 10 percent success rate common in the 1800s, it is roughly equivalent when one considers the Graham inquirer has numerous exposures to the Gospel and personal counseling, equivalent to an 1800s inquirer attending an after-meeting and then a minister visiting him at home until God deigned to save him.

According to Kel Richards, National Coordinator for BGEA Australia, on the 1994 Christian Life and Witness Course video made for Australian BGEA counselors, only 2 percent of conversions take place during the sermon, 48 percent during counseling and 50 percent sometime during follow-up. When the previously cited 25 percent salvation rate is applied to these statistics, Graham's formula for success looks even better. If only a sermon is provided, just one half of one percent of decisions will be effective. If a sermon plus altar counseling is provided, twelve and a half percent of decisions will be effective. If a sermon plus altar counseling plus follow-up is provided, twenty-five percent of decisions for Christ will be effective.

Counseling and Follow-up

Every pastor and evangelist needs to listen to Billy Graham: "I don't believe any man can come to Christ unless the Holy Spirit has prepared his heart. Second, I don't believe any man can come to Christ unless God draws him. My job is to proclaim the message. It's the Holy Spirit's job to do the work. And so I approach it with a great deal of relaxation now.

"There's the moment of conception, there's nine months of gestation, there is birth. Now I believe that these people who come forward in our meetings to make a commitment, for some it is a moment of conception, for others it's another stage in gestation, for others it is birth into the Kingdom of God. And for many it's completely spurious and there's nothing to it."[2] (my italics)

The period from conception to being "born again" is a "stage of gestation" (or struggle of faith) that can last for days, weeks, months or even years. Graham explained this spiritual phenomenon in his book, *Peace With God*: "Not all conversions come as a sudden, brilliant flash of soul illumination that we call a crisis conversion. There are many others that are accomplished only after a long and difficult conflict with the inner motives of the person. With others, conversion comes at the climactic moment of a long period of a gradual conviction of their need and revelation of the plan of salvation. This prolonged process results in conscious acceptance of Christ as personal Savior and in the yielding of life to Him. We may say therefore, that conversion can be an instantaneous event, a crisis in which the person receives a clear revelation of the love of God; or it can be a gradual unfoldment accompanied by a climactic moment at the time the line is crossed between darkness and light, between death and life everlasting."[3]

As stated earlier, Graham said in an interview with David Frost that only a fourth of the decisions at his crusades result in people being eventually born again: "The parable of the sower, in which Jesus indicated that there were four types of soil that the Word of God lands on. And a fourth of those are, will go on to grow in the grace and knowledge of Christ and become true disciples, but three fourths of those will not. ... I've always thought in any group that comes forward to make a commitment, if I've preached the Gospel faithfully, a fourth of them will be there five years from now or ten years from now."[4]

Regarding three-fourths of the people who came to the altar and made a decision for Christ, Graham said they would not be born again even with excellent counseling and extended follow-up. Regarding the remaining one fourth, many had to go through a struggle of faith before being saved, which made excellent counseling and extended follow-up absolutely essential.

Graham insisted on a maximum effort from counselors and participating churches. Counselors were to contact inquirers after the crusade within forty-eight hours, church ministers were to visit their homes, and Bible study programs were to begin immediately.

"I disavow any responsibility if the follow-up program cannot be handled by the ministers and the churches."[5]

"I have come to the conclusion that the most important phase is the follow-up."[6]

"The 5 per cent effort to win men to a personal committal to Christ is over: The 95 per cent effort to bring them to maturity in the fellowship of the churches is about to begin."[7]

With this in mind, Graham asked Dawson Trotman three times to use his Navigators' experience to improve crusade counseling and follow-up. Trotman was no lover of mass evangelism. He had learned from experience to "never lead a person in a decision unless he was prepared to adequately follow him up."[8]

Trotman, who worked a short time for Graham until he died trying to save someone from drowning, had come to the conclusion that most decisions were useless without concerted follow-up.

This was a tacit acknowledgement that most twentieth century conversions were not conversions at all, but rather, at best, the beginning of illumination. Trotman strengthened Graham's counseling and follow-up program. The improved follow-up program was supposed to help ministers keep in close contact with seekers who might already be saved, or if only illuminated, (the gestation period mentioned by Graham), hopefully get born again somewhere down the road.

Crossing the Line

Graham describes the point at which one is born again as "crossing the line."[9]

In describing his wife's conversion, he said, "My wife, for example, cannot remember the exact day or hour when she became a Christian, but she is certain that there was such a moment in her life, a moment when she actually crossed the line."[10]

Ruth Bell Graham, like many heroes of the faith, had to go through a struggle of faith. This was the common experience before Billy Sunday changed the salvation paradigm. Most penitents went through days, weeks, months or even years before fully repenting and being born again. [11]

Struggle of Faith Hall of Fame

I wish there were space here to mention briefly the thousands of biographies of Christians who "repented of dead works" when God saved them. Some were saved out of ignorance of the Gospel. Others were saved despite the "form of godliness" of their time. Just being raised in a moral culture didn't make the struggle any easier. In fact, for many, knowing the truth made their struggle all the more painful.

Many like Franklin Graham were raised in Christian homes, went to church and lived seemingly moral lives that would put most of us to shame. Despite their attempts to please God, they knew they were not saved, lacking power over sin and exhibiting no evidence of the works of the Holy Spirit within.

Most great men and women of God had to go through a struggle of faith before receiving salvation. Their struggle of faith began when they became concerned for the welfare of their soul and ended when they knew they were born again. In the case of children raised in Christian homes who always wanted to please God, their struggle of faith is reckoned here as beginning at twelve years of age.

John Calvin's struggle of faith lasted twelve years; George

Fox—twelve years; John Wesley—twenty-three years; George Whitefield—ten years; Jonathan Edwards—five years; David Brainerd—nine years; John Newton—six years; Peter Cartwright—one year; Charles Spurgeon—four years. Virtually every account before 1900 of the born-again experience is characterized by a period of illumination and a struggle of faith.

Spurgeon provides a classic example of the difference between having knowledge *about* salvation and *experiencing* salvation. "For years, as a child, I tried to learn the way of salvation; and either I did not hear it set forth, which I think cannot quite have been the case, or else I was spiritually blind and deaf, and could not see it and could not hear it. ... had I read my Bible? Yes, and read it earnestly. Had I never been taught by Christian people? Yes, I had, by mother, and father, and others. Had I not heard the gospel? Yes I think I had; and yet, somehow, it was like a new revelation to me."[12]

Billy Graham's Struggle of Faith

Billy Graham himself had to go through a struggle of faith. At age fifteen, he attended most of the eleven weeks of meetings held by evangelist Mordecai Ham. He suffered under "'a tremendous conviction that I must commit myself. I'm sure," he recalls, "the Lord did speak to me about certain things in my life. I'm certain of that. But I cannot remember what they were. But I do remember a great sense of burden that I was a sinner before God and had a great fear of hell and judgment."[13]

For more than two months, Graham was convicted, "Yet the price of Christ's friendship would be total surrender for a life-long discipleship; Billy would no longer be his own master. That price he was not yet prepared to pay. When Ham invited those who would accept Christ to move toward the pulpit in an act of witness and definition, Billy Graham stayed in his seat."[14]

Finally, after his sixteenth birthday, he repented and crossed the line. He knew for the first time in his life the workings of the Holy Spirit and power over sin. But because of the phenomenon called "Sunday conversions" (most conversions inspired by evangelists since Billy Sunday were not long-lived), Graham asked himself, "I wonder if this will last?"[15] But in the following months, the changes in his appetites and morality assured him without a doubt that he was born again.

Graham Originates the Public Group Prayer

When Graham started his ministry, he instructed his altar workers to counsel and pray one-on-one with inquirers. John Pollock, Graham biographer, explained the reason: "Each inquirer is an individual, with an individual problem. A counselor must be patient and a good listener, must learn how to point to Christ, and be spiritually alert. ... Before they part, inquirer and counselor pray together and the counselor fills in a card."[16]

When the prayer was done one-on-one like this, the counselor presumably determined the spiritual condition of the penitent, so the prayer could be done in the hope it came from a repentant heart.

Dan Pitt, a BGEA counselor trainer, likened the repeating of a salvation prayer to a marriage vow.

"Not until he stands before witnesses, bends his will to hers, and says, 'I do!'—only at that moment, and not before, is that man married. ... So the counselor who is sitting with Jane Doe asks her friendly, probing questions to make certain that she is genuinely committing herself to Christ, and when the answer is clear the moment is sealed with a short prayer."[17]

The salvation prayer is useful if it comes spontaneously from a heart illuminated by the Holy Spirit. If the prayer is repeated merely because the inquirer is told it will seal their marriage to God, it can cause more harm than good. Gifted counselors look for supernatural impartation. As Lorne Sanny emphasized in BGEA training courses,

"As you talk with a person there is that certain point where God takes over, and causes the light to shine, and a miracle takes place."[18]

Contrary to popular opinion, Billy Graham never believed everyone who repeated a salvation prayer was saved. He acknowledged: "Some were following the whim of temporary emotion, some did not realize what they were doing."[19] More importantly, he only reluctantly started the practice of leading large groups in a salvation prayer because he didn't have enough trained counselors to handle the crush of people.[20] It was only later that this time-saving device became acceptable as normal procedure for an altar call.

The First Innovation:
Public Group Prayer *after* Counseling

As discussed earlier, the first way Graham used the salvation prayer was one-on-one in the privacy of the inquiry room *after* counseling. This gave altar workers the ability to sort out whether penitents understood what they were doing before "getting married." Unfortunately, Graham felt the need to streamline the process. Curtis Mitchell, in *Those Who came Forward*, explains why Graham changed the custom: "In smaller crusades, this prayer was made within the walls of an adjacent inquiry room, but as crowds of converts grew larger, *it became Graham's custom to lead it himself* and to end the counseling session *in the open*."[21] (my italics)

Graham's leading the prayer at the end of the counseling session with large groups in the open was a radical departure from previous procedure. It forever changed the perception of the prayer. No longer was the prayer seen as part of a supernatural impartation between saints, where the counselor served as a midwife to a new birth. (Pollock used the term, "spiritual obstetrician."[22]) Now the prayer was understood mostly as a profession of faith before the world.

The Second Innovation:
Public Group Prayer *before* Counseling

As crowds coming to the altar grew even larger, so did the need for counselors. If there weren't enough counselors, some of the inquirers got away before they could be led in the prayer. One counselor commented: "I found myself surrounded by hundreds of anxious souls, needing instruction and guidance in the Word, while the absence of personal workers was appalling. ... I trembled at seeing scores leaving without anyone to speak to them."[23]

Graham, out of perceived necessity, started doing the group prayer *before* the counseling session. Curtis Mitchell described this second innovation: "The evangelist leans forward to greet inquirers ... he says he will not keep them long. ... And then he leads them all in a unique prayer of confession and repentance, pausing after each phrase to allow them to repeat his simple but explicit words. ... *After the prayer* ... the counseling begins at once."[24] (my italics)

The Problem

Because the Graham Formula provides counseling and follow-up, the system can, in many cases, overcome the inherent dishonesty of telling all inquirers they are born again. But what about the thousands of evangelists and pastors who use the altar call and group salvation prayer without offering counseling and follow-up?

They don't know what Billy Graham said about stages of gestation and getting a decision being only 5 percent of the work. All they know is having inquirers walk to the altar and repeat a salvation prayer is the quickest and easiest way to get a conversion.

History has repeated itself. Billy Sunday took the effective methods of Charles Finney and stripped them of the safeguard of effective counseling, and, in the process, changed the meaning of coming forward in an altar call from seeking salvation to being saved by virtue of the act.

Modern ministers took the effective methods of Billy Graham and stripped them of the safeguard of effective counseling and extended follow-up, and, in the process, changed the meaning of repeating a salvation prayer from a first step in wanting to live for Christ to an irrevocable legal contract by which God is bound—while the inquirer remains a free agent.

Ministers before Graham never used a spoken salvation

prayer precisely because they knew it would encourage inquirers to trust in an external act, as had happened with water baptism. Graham probably wouldn't have instituted the spoken prayer had he known the way it would be used by his successors.

Like Finney, Graham understood the deceitfulness of the human heart and knew the salvation prayer was a useful tool only if saving faith were possible either at the moment of the prayer or in subsequent counseling and follow-up. If saving faith was not present, leading someone in a salvation prayer could be worse than useless. In a 1959 crusade, there were not enough counselors to handle the crowd that swarmed the altar, so Graham told the crowd:

"If you want to give your life to Christ, go home and drop me a letter in the mail and we'll send you follow-up literature that will help you in your Christian life."[25]

But since 1959, the salvation prayer has taken on sacramental status. In the July, 2005 Charisma magazine, Billy Graham was the subject of the editorial by J. Lee Grady. He praised Graham for being "an anchor of integrity" and bemoaned the fact that universalism is taught in some churches. He said essentially that people need to repent and say a sinner's prayer to become Christian and called this old-fashioned conversion.[26]

Perhaps Mr. Grady doesn't know that Billy Graham, the inventor of the salvation prayer system, believes this:

"Just coming forward does not save your soul. It must be an outward manifestation of an inward feeling."[28] "Not only is repentance needed but faith—and this word faith means more than just belief."[27] "We give the people an opportunity to decide 'yes' or 'no.' But the actual conversion must be of God."[29]

"Billy Graham did not claim that all the thousands of inquirers were born again, but 'their interest had been aroused and their conscience had been pricked.'"[30] Graham agreed with D.L. Moody, who warned against an enthusiastic mood, rather than the Spirit of God, causing spurious conversions[31] when he said, "Of those who come forward, some are like the seeds that fall on barren ground and are eaten by wild fowl; some encounter a soil too hard to receive their roots; some alight among weeds so thick that their life is choked."[32]

Billy Graham said he expected a 25 percent born-again rate among those who made a decision for Christ at his crusades. These superb results were only possible because of excellent sermons, competent counseling and extended follow-up. It's easy to understand why ministers that offer only a sermon before the prayer are the source of so many spurious conversions.

The Evangelical Sacrament

The year was 1988. Mary McDonald placed her hand on the TV and was led by Jimmy Swaggart in a salvation prayer. "There's a new name written down in glory," he said as he pointed at her through the screen. She turned off the set and stood wondering, "Is that all there is to it?"

The next day she went to early mass, said the rosary and lit a candle for her husband in Purgatory. At work, she shared her experience with her friend, Sally.

"Oh, that's great, Mary! I'm so glad you've found the Lord!"

"But I don't feel any different. Is something supposed to change?"

"No, you're saved because the Bible says you're saved. It has nothing to do with feelings. The Bible says we are to 'walk by faith.'"

"OK. I get it. It's because I said the prayer that I'm saved."

"Yes. You see, going to church and doing good deeds can't save us; only the blood of Jesus can save us."

"So everything I did before to please God didn't do any good ... but now that I've said the prayer, God is happy with me?"

Sally could see she wasn't getting through. She remembered she had a book at home called *What Does it Mean to be Born Again?* and promised to give it to her the next day.

That night, Sally read the book just to make sure there wasn't any anti-Catholic content. It was written by John Wesley White, an evangelist who worked for Billy Graham. While reading, Sally tried to put herself in the place of a Catholic who didn't understand salvation by faith. When she got to page forty-three, she found just what she was looking for.

"I was conducting a crusade in Middle America one night when Judy, the sixteen-year-old daughter of the Lutheran minister there, came forward to receive Christ. Her father was the chairman of the crusade. Baptized and confirmed, according to her own testimony, she had not yet been born again in Christ until that night."[1]

"Oh, this is GOOOOD," Sally exclaimed as she continued to read.

"In another crusade in the Midwest the whole confirmation class of Holy Trinity Lutheran Church came forward to make decisions for Christ because, as their minister said, they wanted, like Martin Luther, to be sure they were genuinely born again–not just confirmed into the church." [2]

"That nails it," thought Sally as she determined to read the excerpt to her friend. The next day, during their lunch break, Sally read the two salvation examples to Mary.

"Well, do you understand now?"

Mary seemed confused, unable to answer.

"What's the matter?" asked Sally. "Do you understand now that salvation comes by faith?"

Mary slowly formed the words, careful not to hurt her friend's feelings.

"I understand that the sixteen-year-old had a definite born-again experience, because she said so ... but the whole confirmation class assumed they were born again because they went forward. In other words, they went forward because they thought it would save them, and the writer assumed they were born again because they went forward. I thought faith was something on the inside. Why did the author of the book assume they were born again?"

Sally couldn't understand the question. Like the author of the book, she equated going forward with saving faith. Somehow, Sally couldn't see the Lutherans going through the process of confirmation and the Lutherans going forward in an altar call as only *possible* signs of saving faith. And if you, dear reader, can't see the inconsistency, perhaps you too equate going forward and repeating a salvation prayer with salvation ... the evangelical sacrament.

Billy Sunday Evangelism Hits The Fan

This following story is based on an event that took place at a Southern Baptist Church in Missouri in 2003.

Two teenagers walked down the steps of the church gymnasium complex. The seventeen-year-old girl asked her younger brother, "What do you think about the message tonight?"

"I don't know. ... Did the youth pastor mean suicide when he said 'you can even take your own life and not lose your salvation?'"

"Yeah, that's what he meant. I've got a really bad feeling about this. I'm going to tell Dad."

As they drove into the driveway, their mother and father were sitting on the front porch. The boy jumped out of the car and ran to his parents. Father stood up and smiled. "So, how was the youth meeting? ... What was the sermon about?"

"Suicide!" the boy blurted out before his sister could get there. She looked at her brother with a pained expression, grabbed her father's arm and pushed him back into the chair.

"Dad, sit down; I've got to talk to you."

"What happened?"

"The youth pastor said it was OK to kill yourself. I mean, he said God wouldn't hold it against you–that God would still let you into heaven even if you killed yourself."

"Whoa ... hold on ... slow down ... he told *you* this, or did he tell the whole group?"

"It was in his sermon dad. Everybody heard it."

The father sat silently for a moment.

"Sit down kids. Let me explain something. We're Southern Baptists. Part of what we believe is if someone is truly born again, there's no way he can lose his salvation."

The girl couldn't contain herself. She stood up and threw her arms in the air. "But a saved person wouldn't kill himself!"

"Hold on. I've got a problem with that too, but there's another issue ... saying a saved person can kill himself is like saying it's all right to sin because God can't do anything about it. That message might be appropriate if you're making a point of theology with someone you know is saved, but I know most of the kids in your youth meeting. How many would you say are saved?"

"Maybe five–ten at the most."

"And how many were there tonight?"

"About eighty; it was a big crowd There were about fifteen kids I never saw before."

"Whoa ... this is serious. How many of the kids think they're saved?"

"Well, I don't know anything about the fifteen. But *all* our kids *think* they're saved ... because they've all prayed the sinner's prayer."

"So fifteen from eighty is sixty-five. Out of the sixty-five, you think at the most, ten are saved ... that leaves fifty-five kids that probably aren't saved. And these kids were assured by the youth pastor that they could sin, even kill themselves, and God has to take them into heaven. Whatever happened to 'the fear of the Lord is the beginning of wisdom?'"

Jesus warned of hell repeatedly, and cautioned, "Unless your righteousness surpasses that of the scribes and Pharisees, you will not enter the kingdom of heaven" (Matthew 5:20 NASB). An effective presentation of the Gospel must start with the fear of the Lord. Almost every sermon Jesus preached warned of judgment for sin as the motive for being "perfect, even as your Father which is in heaven is perfect" (Matthew 5:48). The purpose of almost every parable was to warn of inevitable destruction if the listeners didn't repent.

In the book of Matthew, in addition to the parables, the message of Jesus clearly warns of the consequences of sin in 243 verses, compared to just 61 verses centered on the blessings of serving God. His message was clear from His first sermon on earth: "Repent ye: for the kingdom of heaven is at hand" (Matthew 3:2), till His last sermon from heaven, "I come quickly; and my reward is with me, to give every man according as his work" (Revelation 22:12).

God-Given Repentance

The definition of repentance is somewhat alien to modern American thinking. After one hundred years of modern theology, most Americans have a "sloppy agape" understanding of serving God. The bumper sticker "I'M NOT PERFECT–JUST FORGIVEN" sums up American pop Christianity.

Elvis, Willie Nelson and Bill Clinton were *supposed* to be born again. I'm told that even the publisher of the pornographic magazine *Hustler* is a born again Christian! Spurgeon warned us: "Brethren, are any of you that profess to be God's servants living for yourselves? Then you are not God's servants; for he that is really born again lives unto God: the object of his life is the glory of God and the good of his fellow-men." [1]

John the Baptist and Repentance

Modern Americans are just the latest in a long line of people trying to escape judgment without repentance.

"You brood of vipers, who warned you to flee from the wrath to come?" John the Baptist told the Pharisees and Sadducees coming for baptism, "Therefore bear fruit in keeping with repentance; and do not suppose that you can say to yourselves, 'We have Abraham for our father'; for I say to you, that from these stones God is able to raise up children to Abraham." (Matthew 3:7-9 NASB).

When John the Baptist saw the religious leaders coming to get in on the forgiveness his baptism symbolized, he warned them not to be deceived. He was aware of the importance of repentance and understood it wasn't possible for these religious leaders to repent, lacking God-given faith. Many of these Pharisees and Sadducees believed John the Baptist was a true prophet. They wanted to be baptized. But something was wrong. The prophet would not baptize them. Why? He discerned that the hearts of the Pharisees and Sadducees were not right–not repentant.

If John the Baptist refused the Pharisees and Sadducees out of concern for their souls–not wanting them to have the false hope that God had forgiven them, thus, encouraging them to continue in sin, how much more should we be concerned?

Why is Repentance Necessary?

Repentance is the cross, the intersection where God's law and God's mercy work together to bring about the ultimate goal of reconciling man to God. Repentance can only occur if God illuminates the seeker to his true condition. In fact, repentance without God-given faith to overcome the sin being repented of is a mockery of true salvation. It's like a harlot walking down the aisle with a holy man. She wears a white dress to symbolize imaginary purity, accepts a ring symbolizing imaginary submission and says a meaningless marriage vow. "Through sickness and in health, for richer or for poorer, till death do us part" are repeated as part of the ceremony, but it's a mockery.

Water Baptism and Repentance

The early church understood water baptism as a kind of marriage ceremony that united the believer and Christ. Instead of walking down the aisle with a white dress, the believer willingly goes under the water to die with Jesus on the cross (Romans 6:3-7; Galatians 2:20; Galatians 5:24; Galatians 6:14; John 3:29; 2 Corinthians 11:2; Ephesians 5:27).

The bride must die to her old life before she can be married to God. This death pact binds the two together in complete unity, making it possible for Jesus and the believer to become one spirit (1 Corinthians 6:17). When a believer accepts the sacrifice, he identifies with, (becomes one with) all the transforming power of that event.

"Therefore we are buried with him by baptism into death: that like as Christ was raised up from the dead by the glory of the Father, even so we also should walk in newness of life" (Romans 6:4).

"...if the Spirit of him that raised up Jesus from the dead dwell in you, he that raised up Christ from the dead shall also quicken your mortal bodies by his Spirit that dwelleth in you" (Romans 8:11).

Charles Finney on Repentance

Finney spoke more on the subject of repentance than any other evangelist for he knew his methods would produce an unacceptable number of "false appearances" without it.

Here are some of the things he taught about awakened sinners: "Many think that remorse, a sense of guilt, is repentance. Then hell is full of repentance, because it is full of unutterable, eternal remorse. Others feel regret over something and call that repentance.

But they regret their sin because of consequences, not because they hate sin. This isn't repentance. Others believe conviction of sin and strong fears of hell are repentance; they claim they never do anything wrong without repenting–and they always feel sorry for it. Show sinners that none of these things are repentance. They are entirely consistent with the utmost evil–the devil could have them all and yet remain a devil. Repentance is a change of mind regarding sin itself."[2]

Here are some of the things he taught about new converts:

"I don't need to run around informing new converts that they are converted. If a person has obeyed God, he will know it. Telling someone 'You're converted' before he discovers that fact himself easily breeds false hope. It is usually best to let the hope or belief that he is converted spring spontaneously from the young converts own mind."[3]

Finney said, "Willing and wanting are two different things. People often want to be Christians when they don't will to be. When we see anything that looks good to us, we naturally want it–we can't help wanting it in proportion to its goodness. But we can still be unwilling to have it, all things considered."[4]

True Repentance Requires Faith

True repentance is evident when the penitent knows he cannot live without God's personal help. This help is called "grace." Grace is not forgiveness of past sin only; it is the power of God to not sin again. Therefore, repentance depends on the grace of God.

The power of God to forgive sin and the power of God to keep the penitent out of the very sin he repented of is an evidence of salvation. This is the inevitable result of being raised from the dead with Christ by the indwelling Holy Spirit.

In the parable of the seed, the condition of the soil, men's hearts, determined whether the seed would bear fruit. Jesus taught that only a portion would be saved. Nevertheless, we must continue to teach seekers about the fear of the Lord, sin, judgment, the law and the way of salvation while we encourage them to seek God.

"The Lord is not slow about His promise, as some count slowness, but is patient toward you, not wishing for any to perish but for all to come to repentance" (2 Peter 3:9 NASB).

The Bride of Christ

Paul said to the Corinthians, "I have espoused you to one husband, that I may present you as a chaste virgin to Christ" (2 Corinthians 11:2).

"For this cause shall a man leave his father and mother, and shall be joined unto his wife, and they two shall be one flesh. This is a great mystery: but I speak concerning Christ and the church" (Ephesians 5:31-32).

While in this case Paul was speaking of the corporate body being the Bride of Christ, there are many instances where he used marriage language to describe individual saints being *in* Christ and Christ being *in* saints.

"Examine yourselves, whether ye be in the faith; prove your own selves. Know ye not your own selves, how that Jesus Christ is *in* you, except ye be reprobates" (2 Corinthians 13:5).

"What? know ye not that your body is the temple of the Holy Ghost which is *in* you, which ye have of God, and ye are not your own" (1 Corinthians 6:19).

"What? know ye not that he which is joined to an harlot is one body? For two, saith he, shall be one flesh. But he that is joined unto the Lord is *one spirit*" (1 Corinthians 6:16-17).

I'm in Christ, and Christ's in Me

It is no coincidence that the path to wholeness offered by modern psychology is the opposite of that prescribed in the Bible. "YOU DESERVE A BREAK TODAY" and "LOVE THYSELF" are typical expressions of a culture that doesn't understand the Way, the Truth and the Life as freedom. There has never been an earthly marriage as intimate as the marriage between the Christian and Christ by the Holy Spirit. The saint who is one spirit with God has a life filled with purpose and meaning and should have no problem with low self-esteem.

Therapists convince their patients guilt has nothing to do with sin and teach the key to wholeness is "self-realization." Solomon called this foolishness.

"A fool hath no delight in understanding, but that his heart may discover itself" (Proverbs 18:2).

The worst part of modern psychology is it "works" as long as, like Dorothy in the Wizard of Oz, the adherent keeps repeating, "There's no place like home; there's no place like home." Unfortunately, when the poor unfortunate dies, there'll be the devil to pay.

The saint, on the other hand, knows the Truth by faith.

"Although the fig tree shall not blossom, neither shall fruit be in the vines; the labour of the olive shall fail, and the fields shall yield no meat; the flock shall be cut off from the fold, and there shall be no herd in the stalls: Yet I will rejoice in the Lord, I will joy in the God of my salvation. The Lord God is my strength, and he will make my feet like hinds' feet, and he will make me to walk upon mine high places" (Habakkuk 3:17-19).

"Who shall separate us from the love of Christ? Shall tribulation, or distress, or persecution, or famine, or nakedness, or peril, or sword? As it is written, For thy sake we are killed all the day long; we are accounted as sheep for the slaughter. Nay, in all these things we are more than conquerors through him that loved us. For I am persuaded, that neither death, nor life, nor angels, nor principalities, nor powers, nor things present, nor things to come, Nor height, nor depth, nor any other creature, shall be able to separate us from the love of God, which is in Christ Jesus our Lord" (Romans 8:35-39).

The indwelling Christ enabled the early Christians to walk into a gladiator arena singing praises to God minutes before being eaten by wild beasts.

Christ in you is all you need:

"For ye are dead, and *your life is hid with Christ in God*" (Colossians 3:3).

"...this mystery among the Gentiles; which is *Christ in you, the hope of glory*" (Colossians 1:27).

"Even the Spirit of truth; whom the world cannot receive, because it seeth him not, neither knoweth him: but *ye know him; for he dwelleth with you, and shall be in you*" (John 14:17).

"If a man love me, he will keep my words: and my Father will love him, and *we will come unto him, and make our abode with him*" (John 14:23).

And you are in Christ:

"There is therefore now no condemnation to *them which are in Christ Jesus*, who walk not after the flesh, but after the Spirit" (Romans 8:1).

"For the law of the *Spirit of life in Christ Jesus hath made me free* from the law of sin and death" (Romans 8:2).

"But of him are *ye in Christ Jesus,* who of God is made unto us wisdom, and righteousness, and sanctification, and redemption" (1 Corinthians 1:30).

"Therefore *if any man be in Christ, he is a new creature*: old things are passed away; behold, all things are become new" (2 Corinthians 5:17).

As E.M.B. Green said, "Without the twofold solidarity of God with us in Christ, and of us with Christ in God, the New Testament doctrine of justification, so far from establishing God's righteousness, would be immoral. As it is, there is no question of 'legal fiction,' for believers are in Christ, and share His status of righteousness. ... How faith like that can be construed as something sub-personal defeats me!"[1]

The New Covenant in Christ

In the old covenant, Israel was asked to keep the Law solely by human effort, without any outside spiritual help other than the written and spoken Word. Except for anointed priests, prophets and kings, the people of Israel were not given a measure of God's Spirit.

In this desperate state, still in the bondage of corruption (Romans 8:21), the children of Adam didn't fulfill the requirements of the Law. The Law served as a schoolmaster to show man the utter impossibility of pleasing God in one's own strength. The Law could not be kept without God's intimate help.

So Israel was brought to the point of despair.

"O wretched man that I am! Who shall deliver me from the body of this death?" (Romans 7:24).

"Christ hath redeemed us from the curse of the law ... that we might receive the promise of the Spirit through faith" (Galatians 3:13-14).

"For this is the covenant that I will make with the house of Israel after those days, saith the Lord; I will put my laws into their mind, and write them in their hearts" (Hebrews 8:10).

"But the Comforter, which is the Holy Ghost, whom the Father will send in my name, he shall teach you all things, and bring all things to your remembrance, whatsoever I have said unto you" (John 14:26).

"But the anointing which ye have received of him abideth in you, and ye need not that any man teach you: but as the same anointing teacheth you of all things, and is truth, and is no lie, and even as it hath taught you, ye shall abide in him" (1 John 2:27).

"They that are after the flesh do mind the things of the flesh; but they that are after the Spirit the things of the Spirit" (Romans 8:5).

Jesus was the First of His Kind

The Holy Spirit came upon Jesus immediately after He was baptized. He promised the same thing would happen to his followers (Acts 1:5).

Peter repeated the promise when he preached, "Be baptized every one of you in the name of Jesus Christ for the remission of sins, and ye shall receive the gift of the Holy Ghost" (Acts 2:38).

Peter remembered the promise again when explaining why he baptized Gentiles (Acts 11:16).

John the Baptist had prophesied that Jesus would completely immerse believers in the Holy Ghost (Matthew 3:11; Mark 1:8; Luke 3:16; John 1:33).

Jesus told Nicodemus that only those born of the Spirit would enter the kingdom of God (John 3:5).

The apostle John said matter-of-factly that those who believed on Jesus would receive the Holy Ghost, calling Him "rivers of living water" (John 7:38-39).

Later, Jesus promised the disciples that the Father would send the Holy Spirit to believers in His name (John 14:26).

This is how it would be possible for the disciples to be one with God as Jesus and the Father were one (John 17:21).

When God consummates his marriage with a believer, the Holy Spirit gives him a new nature, new power over sin, and a new name (saint), which is the same as the Holy Spirit's name ... that name is "holy" (Strong's 40).

When Paul came upon the disciples of Apollos, "He said unto them, Have ye received the Holy Ghost since ye believed? And they said unto him, We have not so much as heard whether there be any Holy Ghost. And he said unto them, Unto what then were ye baptized? And they said, Unto John's baptism" (Acts 19:2-3).

Notice in Paul's mind the connection between water baptism and receiving the Holy Ghost. Also, he equated "believing" with water baptism. The Holy Spirit is the agent of salvation.

Paul knew something was wrong with the disciples of Apollos. Perhaps they didn't exhibit "righteousness, and peace, and joy in the Holy Ghost" (Romans 14:17). Perhaps they never mentioned the name of Jesus ... a pretty good indication that He wasn't inside of them (2 Corinthians 13:5). Whatever the reason, Paul assumed when they were baptized correctly as a function of saving faith in Christ, they would receive the Holy Spirit ... and they did.

The Definition of Marriage and Salvation

In order to understand how the meaning of New Testament salvation evolved, let's compare it to the evolution of the definition of human marriage. One hundred years ago, western civilization saw marriage as a union between a man and a woman. Becoming "one flesh" took place at the consummation of the marriage when a man and a woman had sexual intercourse. For example, Rebecca was betrothed to Isaac from the time she said "I will" to Abraham's servant, but she married—became one flesh with—Isaac (without the benefit of a ceremony) soon after she entered his tent (Genesis 24:67).

If a man raped a maid, he was forced to give her all the privileges of a wife (Exodus 22:16), since he had married her.

In ancient Roman, it was illegal for a couple to marry unless they could consummate the marriage through sexual intercourse.

A man without a functional penis was not allowed to marry. The Roman law allowed all eunuchs to make wills (Code of Justinian 6.22.5, 12.5.4.2-3) and perform guardianship duties (Code of Justinian 5.62.1). But only whole eunuchs (men for whom sexual intercourse was psychologically difficult, but physically possible), were eligible for marriage (D 23.3.39.1, 28.2.6). In the first century, Jewish men born with missing or deformed genitals were prevented from getting married.[2]

In the New Testament, Jesus referred to eunuchs as those that didn't marry, either by choice or because of physical impossibility. Those that chose not to marry for the sake of the kingdom of God were called eunuchs because being a eunuch was the same as "one who couldn't, or chose not to engage in sex" (Matthew 19:12). In other words, there was no such thing as a marriage that couldn't be consummated.

This may be hard for us to understand, but remember, the only thing that distinguishes a marriage from all other relationships–including family relationships, is that the couple engages in sexual intercourse and can potentially reproduce.

Fast-forward 2,000 years. Marriage has been divorced from heterosexual sex. Marriage is now a state of mind. If two or more people want to "get married," their state of mind is all that matters.

Now let's look at how the definition of New Testament salvation has changed in exactly the same way. Modern evangelism theology defines salvation as a state of mind. If you want to be saved, and say the right words, you are saved. It doesn't matter that your marriage with God hasn't been consummated. It's irrelevant whether or not the Holy Spirit has come into you, making you one spirit with Christ (1 Corinthians 6:17). All that matters is that you *think* you're saved.

The Two Yardsticks of Salvation

One hundred years ago, pastors and evangelists had the two yardsticks with which to measure salvation. These were "power over sin" and "the workings of the Holy Spirit" in the individual. Today, few evangelical ministers rely on these two evidences in counseling church members. After 100 years of evolving evangelical theology, the question of whether someone is able to resist sin is considered a psychological problem, not a salvation problem. Thus, the power over sin, the most visible evidence of salvation ("by their fruits ye shall know them" [Matthew 7:20; Jude 1:12; John 15:5; Romans 7:4-5; Romans 6:22; Galatians 5:22-24; Ephesians 5:9]), has largely become a moot point.

Many pastors and evangelists, in part because of the rise of Pentecostalism, are also reluctant to recognize the *second* evidence of salvation. If you read the writings of Baptists, Methodists, Presbyterians, etc. before 1900, you find continual references to the working of the Holy Spirit in Christians. After 1900, however, the writings become increasingly silent on this essential subject.

Now, more times than not, Christian counselors are ignorant of the wealth of biblical insight on the workings of the Holy Spirit in the Christian. The Reformers recognized the workings of the Holy Spirit as the way a person is saved and changed from glory to glory. Much of evangelical Christianity has largely cut itself off from this foundational truth.

Saints have the Holy Spirit within them

Unlike all other religions, Christianity is not confined to the written word. The true Christian lives *for* God, by living *from* God, moment by moment in the Holy Spirit. The first yardstick of salvation is the working of the Holy Spirit in the saint.
It is in Him we …
1.   … find mental health by being born of the Spirit (John 3:5)
2.   … are quickened by the Spirit (John 6:63)
3.   … are guided by the Spirit (John 16:13)
4.   … walk after the Spirit (Romans 8:1)

5.   ... mind the things of the Spirit (Romans 8:5)
6.   ... are led of the Spirit (Romans 8:14)
7.   ... are adopted in the Spirit (Romans 8:15)
8.   ... receive the witness of the Spirit (Romans 8:16)
9.   ... have the first fruits of the Spirit (Romans 8:23)
10.   ... receive the help of the Spirit (Romans 8:26)
11.   ... understand the intercession of the Spirit (Romans 8:27)
12.   ... understand the things of God through the Spirit
        (1 Corinthians 2:14)
13.   ... become the temple of the Spirit (1 Corinthians 3:16)
14.   ... are washed and sanctified by the Spirit (1 Corinthians 6:11)
15.   ... are made one with God in the Spirit (1 Corinthians 6:17)
16.   ... are made to drink into the Spirit (2 Corinthians 12:13)
17.   ... experience the liberty of the Spirit (2 Corinthians 3:17)
18.   ... are changed from glory to glory by the Spirit
        (2 Corinthians 3:18)
19.   ... experience in our heart the earnest of the Spirit
        (2 Corinthians 5:5)
20.   ... experience the Spirit crying "Abba, Father" in our hearts
        (Galatians 4:6)
21.   ... experience in the Spirit the hope of righteousness by faith
        (Galatians 5:5)
22.   ... experience the fruit of the Spirit (Galatians 5:22)
23.   ... live by the Spirit (Galatians 5:25)
24.   ... sow to the Spirit (Galatians 6:8)
25.   ... reap life everlasting from the Spirit (Galatians 6:8)
26.   ... are sealed with the Spirit (Ephesians 1:13)
27.   ... have access to God by the Spirit (Ephesians 2:18)
28.   ... are made into a suitable house for God in the Spirit
        (Ephesians 2:22)
29.   ... are strengthened in the inner man by the Spirit
        (Ephesians 3:16)
30.   ... are filled with the Spirit (Ephesians 5:18)
31.   ... understand and use the sword of the Spirit
        (Ephesians 6:17)
32.   ... pray in the Spirit (Ephesians 6:18)

33.   ... experience the supply of the Spirit (Philippians 1:19)
34.   ... experience fellowship of the Spirit (Philippians 2:1)
35.   ... worship God in the Spirit (Philippians 3:3)
36.   ... exhibit love in the Spirit (Colossians 1:8)
37.   ... obey the truth through the Spirit (1 Peter 1:22)
38.   ... know God abides inside by the Spirit (1 John 3:24)
39.   ... know we dwell in God and He in us because we have
        the Spirit (1 John 4:13)

Saints Have Power over Sin

The second yardstick of salvation (power over sin) is even *more* obvious than the first.

"Whosoever committeth sin is the servant of sin. ... If the Son therefore shall make you free, ye shall be free indeed." (John 8:34-36).

"For he that is dead is freed from sin" (Romans 6:7).

"For sin shall not have dominion over you" (Romans 6:14).

"Being then made free from sin, ye became the servants of righteousness" (Romans 6:18).

"But now being made free from sin, and become servants to God" (Romans 6:22).

"For the law of the Spirit of life in Christ Jesus hath made me free from the law of sin and death" (Romans 8:2).

"God is faithful, who will not suffer you to be tempted above that ye are able; but will with the temptation also make a way to escape, that ye may be able to bear it" (1 Corinthians 10:13).

"For if we sin wilfully after that we have received the knowl-. edge of the truth, there remaineth no more sacrifice for sins" (Hebrews 10:26)."

"Whosoever is born of God doth not commit sin; for his seed remaineth in him: and he cannot sin, because he is born of God" (1 John 3:9).

Saints can have a Clean Conscience

Because saints have power over sin and the Holy Spirit within them, they can have a clean conscience.

"...my conscience also bearing me witness in the Holy Ghost" (Romans 9:1).

"For our rejoicing is this, the testimony of our conscience" (2 Corinthians 1:12).

"Now the end of the commandment is charity out of a pure heart, and of a good conscience" (1 Timothy 1:5).

"Holding the mystery of the faith in a pure conscience" (1 Timothy 3:9).

"Let us draw near with a true heart in full assurance of faith, having our hearts sprinkled from an evil conscience" (Hebrews 10:22).

"The like figure whereunto even baptism doth also now save us (not the putting away of the filth of the flesh, but the answer of a good conscience toward God)" (1 Peter 3:21).

Saints have No Reason to Fear Death

Because saints have power over sin and the Holy Spirit within them, they can be free from the fear of death.

"And deliver them who through fear of death were all their lifetime subject to bondage" (Hebrews 2:15).

"He that heareth my word, and believeth on him that sent me, hath everlasting life, and shall not come into condemnation; but is passed from death unto life" (John 5:24).

"If a man keep my saying, he shall never taste of death" (John 8:52).

"For I am persuaded, that neither death, nor life ... shall be able to separate us from the love of God, which is in Christ Jesus our Lord" (Romans 8:38-39).

What do you think I am, a Saint?

The Sunday school teachers at Liberty Baptist were having an argument ... er ... a ... no, a *discussion* about unruly kids. Mrs. Ketts was of the opinion that any behavior short of dangerous was acceptable, while Mr. Radi wanted more discipline.

"You must try to understand, Mr. Radi, American kids are not like kids in India."

"I've noticed. They are disrespectful and ignorant. I have never seen such behavior among teenagers before. And these kids are *supposed* to be Christian."

"Mr. Radi, you haven't been here long. ... I mean, in the United States. Being a Christian has nothing to do with it. Perhaps Christians in India are better behaved because *everyone* is better behaved."

"No, Christians in India are better behaved because Christians in India *are Christian*."

"What's that supposed to mean?"

"Mrs. Ketts, be honest with me. How many of the kids in your class do you think are really born again?"

She looked down at the table and sat silently. After a pause during which a person could have gotten up, poured a cup of coffee and returned to his seat, she looked up and said, "If you keep thinking like that, you won't fit in here."

Now it was Mr. Radi who was silent. He couldn't figure out what she meant. Was there a rule about questioning someone's salvation?

Just then the pastor came in. "Sorry I'm late. What did I miss?"

"Mr. Radi just said our teenagers don't act like Christians."

"Oh, well, I guess that's why we need you Mr. Radi–so you can teach them how to act like Christians."

"I'm afraid I cannot take the place of the Holy Spirit. Most of the kids in my class show no sign of being born again."

"Oh? Is this a new doctrine from India? Is there some fool-proof way of knowing who is or isn't a Christian?"

This conversation illustrates the typical, American evangelical attitude toward salvation and behavior. When church kids come back from Bible camp or the sanctuary altar having "given their life to Jesus," we hope for the best and brace for the worse. Our low expectations are consistent with a theology that sees salvation as merely a state of mind, not a supernatural indwelling of the Holy Spirit.

What's A Saint?

All the problems of the "backslidden" state of the evangelical American church can be understood by answering a question: What's a saint? Christians in the New Testament are called sinners only twice. They are called disciples or saints in almost every other instance.

"Saint" was such a common description of Christians that the writers of the New Testament used the word sixty-two times. A saint is nothing more or less than a holy person. The word translated "saint" just means "holy" ("hagios" Strongs 40). It's the exact word used in conjunction with the word for Spirit to make the name Holy Spirit. It's the same word used in Revelation 4:8 when the heavenly host worship God saying, "Holy, holy, holy, Lord God Almighty" It's the same word used by Peter when he said, "He which hath called you is holy, so be ye holy in all manner of conversation; Because it is written, Be ye holy; for I am holy" (1 Peter 1:15-16). As far as the Bible is concerned, Christians are saints, which means Christians are holy.

Holistic or Gnostic Christian?

Starting with the Christian Brethren in Britain in the early nineteenth century, and then spreading through teachers like J.N. Darby, intellectual belief about Christ was increasingly considered to be saving "faith."[1] This radical departure from previous evangelical theology encouraged seekers to believe not on the person of Christ, but in the fact that Christ paid the debt for sin, effectively reducing faith to belief in certain facts. A Methodist minister summed up their teaching as, "You are saved because you believe you are saved."[2]

But knowledge (or "gnosis" in the Greek) is not the same as faith as defined in the Bible. A Gnostic Christian who hasn't repented of sin cannot be saved from the consequences of it. As Charles Finney said, "What good would it do to forgive you while the sin still rules your heart?"[3]

Gnostic Christians in the first century were excluded from fellowship by the Apostles because they excused a lifestyle of sin, saying Christians could sin in their flesh yet remain pure in their spirit. They thought salvation was wholly dependent on personal "knowledge." The Reformers excluded Gnostic Christians in the sixteenth century for the same reason. They were called "antinomians," which means "people against the law." Antinomian Christians believed they were saved regardless of whether or not they kept the laws of God.

When Luther nailed his Ninety-Five Theses to the Wittenberg door, the first four theses refuted Gnosticism. "1. Our Lord and master Jesus Christ is saying 'Repent ye, etc.,' meant the whole life of the faithful to be an act of repentance. 2. This saying cannot be understood of the sacrament of penance (i.e., of confession and absolution), which is administered by the priesthood. 3. Yet He does not mean an interior repentance only; nay, interior repentance is void if it does not externally produce different kinds of mortifications of the flesh. 4. And so penance remains while self-hate remains (i.e., true interior penitence); namely, right up to entrance into the kingdom of heaven."[4]

Romans 7:25 and Carnal Christianity

The most common scripture used to justify Gnostic Christianity is Romans 7:14-25, which ends with, "I thank God through Jesus Christ our Lord. So then with the mind I myself serve the law of God; but with the flesh the law of sin." Up until this point, Paul seemed to be describing the state of an awakened sinner. But then, when he says, "I thank God through Jesus Christ our Lord," it seems like he's saying this despicable condition is that of someone

who is born again. If you look at all of Romans 6, he completely repudiates the notion that a Christian could serve two masters.
"For sin shall not have dominion over you: for ye are not under
the law, but under grace. What then? shall we sin, because we are
not under the law, but under grace? God forbid" (Romans 6:14-15).

Two Ways of Interpreting Romans 7:14-7:25

Most theologians believe Paul was speaking of a born-again
individual in Romans 7:14-7:25. If this is the case, then the huge
caveat described by Luther is necessary to understand how they can
take this shocking position.

"(Paul is) dealing with the Law as it applies to the inner man
and the will and not with respect to the works of the outer man. ...
The apostle's method of speaking are contrary to the metaphysical
or moral methods. For the apostle says what he does in order to indicate (or sound forth) that man rather than sin is taken away, for sin
remains as a kind of relic, and man is purged from sin rather than
the opposite. ... Thus it is obvious that the apostle means that sin is
taken away by a spiritual means (that is, the will to commit sin is put
to death) ... Hence blessed Augustine ... says, 'What are the Laws of
God which He Himself has written in our hearts if they are not the
very presence of the Holy Spirit, who is the finger of God and by
whose presence love is shed abroad in our hearts? And this love is
the fulfilling of the Law and the end of the commandment.'"[5]

Restated in modern language, only by yielding to the Holy
Spirit can the Christian not serve sin. He is powerless in his flesh to
do otherwise. Sin will always have the capacity to rule a Christian
if he doesn't yield to the Holy Spirit within. So, according to Luther
and most famous theologians, Romans 7:14-7:25 doesn't teach the
Gnostic heresy of the acceptability of serving sin in the flesh while
serving God in the spirit. Rather, it teaches the flesh is incapable of
serving God, so the Christian can succeed in life only as he walks by
the power of the Holy Spirit. The clear implication of this teaching
is--if a person is incapable of staying out of habitual sin, then the
Holy Spirit is not present in the individual. In other words, "carnal
Christians" are not saved.

The New Gnosticism

The reason Paul brought us through Romans 7 was to arrive at Romans 8. But many pastors teach a "carnal Christian" interpretation of Romans 7:25. Unlike Paul, Augustine, Luther, Calvin and most evangelical theologians before the twentieth century, they don't teach the holistic salvation of Romans 6 and Romans 8, but teach exactly what Paul said "God forbid" to in Romans 6:15.

The twentieth century forensic atonement doctrine is identical in its effect to the first century Gnostic heresy that a man could sin in his flesh while remaining pure in his spirit.

In commenting on this doctrine, J.I. Packer said, "The pastoral effect of this teaching can only be to produce what the Puritans called 'Gospel hypocrites'—persons who have been told that they are Christians, eternally secure, because they believe that Christ died for them, when their hearts are unchanged and they have no personal commitment to Christ at all. I know this, for I was just such a Gospel hypocrite for two years before God mercifully made me aware of my unconverted state."[6]

Ernest Reisinger said, "As a result of this erroneous teaching many who regularly occupy our church pews on Sunday morning and fill our church rolls are strangers to true conversion. They are strangers to heart religion because they have never experienced the power of a changed life. They are not new creatures and for them old things have not passed away."[7]

What does it mean to "Believe on The Lord Jesus Christ?"

"[He] brought them out, and said, Sirs, what must I do to be saved? And they said, Believe on the Lord Jesus Christ, and thou shalt be saved" (Acts 16:30-31).

This scripture is used in modern evangelism as a formula for instant salvation. Using a single scripture this way is called reductionism–and is bad theology. There are at least seven aspects to salvation including belief, repentance, trust and assurance, commitment and allegiance, water baptism, the gift of the Holy Spirit and incorporation into Christian community.

To say all one needs to do is "believe" to be saved because of what Paul said to the Philippian jailer, is as illogical as saying all one needs to do is be "obedient" to be saved because of what Luke said in Acts 6:7. As Gordon Smith writes in *Beginning Well,*

"When the Bible refers to the conversion experience through one of the components, we must not be reductionist and conclude that particular element is all that's necessary 'to be saved.' While conversion is complex and has many different elements, any one of these elements can represent the whole of the experience."[1]

If one wanted to make an argument for reductionism–and I don't, the *only* salvation element that would fit the bill would be water baptism.

"... baptism now saves you–not the removal of dirt from the flesh, but an appeal to God for a good conscience" (1 Peter 3:21 NASB).

"For as many of you as have been baptized into Christ have put on Christ" (Galatians 3:27).

"Know ye not, that so many of us as were baptized into Jesus Christ were baptized into his death" (Romans 6:3).

Another scripture commonly used in evangelism is Romans 10:9: "If thou shalt confess with thy mouth the Lord Jesus, and shalt believe in thine heart that God hath raised him from the dead, thou shalt be saved." Using this as a reductionist salvation formula ignores the meaning of the scripture in context.

Certainly no one could argue that Paul thought water baptism was superfluous. In fact, Paul insisted on baptizing the very one he told to "believe on the Lord Jesus Christ" (Acts 16:33), and in another place, Paul equated water baptism with believing (Acts 19:2-3).

Water Baptism and Faith are Not Mutually Exclusive

Theologians recognize the existence of what appear to be antinomies in the Bible, but faith and water baptism as the means of salvation is not one of them.

E.M.B. Green said, "The New Testament saw no tension between salvation by faith and salvation by baptism; they are properly regarded as belonging together. ... Paul's own teaching on baptism ... carries with it the implications of dying with Christ and rising to newness of life with Him (Romans 6:1-16), precisely as faith-union with Christ does. And it is the Holy Spirit, given access to the life of the believer when he turns in faith to God for salvation, who actualized in him the death to sin and the life of righteousness of which his baptism speaks. Faith, then, is sealed by the 'outward and visible sign' of baptism, and the 'inward and spiritual grace' of the Holy Spirit received into the life."[2]

Water Baptism is Identifying with Jesus' Sacrifice

One of the primary aspects of baptism is identification with the sacrifice of Christ. Saints need to be *"Buried with him in baptism"* (Colossians 2:12).

Here's what Bible scholars say about baptism:
.

Matthew Henry:
"... not the outward ceremony of washing with water, which, in itself, does no more than put away the filth of the flesh, but it is that baptism wherein there is a faithful answer or restipulation of a resolved good conscience, engaging to believe in, and be entirely devoted to, God ... renouncing at the same time the flesh, the world, and the devil. Washing is the visible sign; this is

the thing signified ... the apostle shows that the efficacy of baptism to salvation depends not upon the work done, but upon the resurrection of Christ, which supposes his death, and is the foundation of our faith and hope, to which we are rendered *conformable by dying to sin, and rising again to holiness and newness of life* ... As Christ suffered in his human nature, do you, according to your baptismal vow and profession, make your corrupt nature suffer, *by putting to death the body of sin by self-denial and mortification; for, if you do thus suffer, you will be conformable to Christ in his death and resurrection, and will cease from sin.*"[3] (my italics)

Barnes:

"... baptism administered in connection with true repentance, and true faith in the Lord Jesus, and when it *is properly a symbol of the putting away of sin, and of the renewing influences of the Holy Spirit, and an act of unreserved dedication* to God–now saves us. *When a man is dead, he will sin no more;' referring of course to the present life. So if a Christian becomes dead in a moral sense-- dead to this world, dead by being crucified with Christ ... he may be expected to cease from sin. The reasoning is based on the idea that there is such a union between Christ and the believer that his death on the cross secured the death of the believer to the world.*"[4] (my italics)

Jamieson, Fausset, and Brown:

"... transferred from the old world to the new ... so we by spiritual baptism ... saves you also, not of itself, but *the spiritual thing conjoined with it, repentance and faith, of which it is the seal, as Peter explains. Compare the union of the sign and thing signified* ...That he (the believer, who has once for all obtained *cessation from sin by suffering, in the person of Christ, namely, in virtue of his union with the crucified Christ) should no longer live the rest of his time in the flesh to the lusts of men, but to the will of God.*"[5] (my italics)

Salvation is Experienced through Death

Paul constantly identifies Christians as dead to sin and the flesh. Just as a Christian was saved, continues to be saved, and will someday be completely saved in the resurrection, so a Christian must have died, continues to die, and will someday completely die to sin and the flesh in the resurrection.

"How shall we, that are *dead* to sin, live any longer therein?" (Romans 6:2).

"For he that is *dead* is freed from sin" (Romans 6:7).

"... if we be *dead* with Christ ... ye also yourselves to be *dead* indeed unto sin" (Romans 6:8-11).

"... if Christ be in you, the body is *dead* because of sin" (Romans 6:10).

"If any man be in Christ, he is a *new creature*: old things are passed away" (2 Corinthians 5:17).

"Wherefore if ye be *dead* with Christ from the rudiments of the world" (Colossians 2:20).

"For ye are *dead*, and your life is hid with Christ in God" (Colossians 3:3).

"... being *dead* to sins" (1 Peter 2:24).

"... so many of us as were baptized into Jesus Christ were baptized into his *death*? ... we are buried with him by baptism into *death*" (Romans 6:3-4).

"... been planted together in the likeness of his *death* ... our old man is *crucified with him*" (Romans 6:5-6).

"For he that is *dead* is freed from sin" (Romans 6:7).

"For we which live are alway delivered unto *death* for Jesus' sake ... *death* worketh in us" (2 Corinthians 4:11-12).

"... being made conformable unto his **death**" (Philippians 3:10).

"For whosoever will save his life shall lose it: and whosoever will *lose his life* for my sake shall find it" (Matthew 16:25).

Many evangelists think they don't have enough time to explain the implicit requirements of the Gospel. Since they don't want to discourage seekers with the truth, they trust in the sacrifice to transform the minds of those who partake of it. In fact, one of the most common appeals to sinners is, "Come as you are, and God will change your heart. Just believe on Jesus, and He'll change you." But what if the seeker's understanding of "believing on Jesus" is only "I believe Jesus paid the price so I can go to heaven, without any requirement on my part." How different this is from the Gospel of Jesus Christ.

"'If anyone comes to Me, and does not hate his own father and mother and wife and children and brothers and sisters, yes, and even his own life, he cannot be My disciple. Whoever does not carry his own cross and come after Me cannot be My disciple. For which one of you, when he wants to build a tower, does not first sit down and calculate the cost to see if he has enough to complete it? Otherwise, when he has laid a foundation and is not able to finish, all who observe it begin to ridicule him, saying, 'This man began to build and was not able to finish.'

Or what king, when he sets out to meet another king in battle, will not first sit down and consider whether he is strong enough with ten thousand men to encounter the one coming against him with twenty thousand? Or else, while the other is still far away, he sends a delegation and asks for terms of peace. So then, none of you can be My disciple who does not give up all his own possessions'" (Luke 14:26-33 NASB).

What is a Sacrifice?

As discussed at length, the Bible teaches that water baptism is identifying with Christ's sacrifice. But most Americans don't know what a sacrifice is. After 100 years of faulty theology, we no longer understand sacrifice as the death of the old life of sin unto a new life of righteousness. Can someone benefit from a sacrifice without knowing what he's partaking of? There is nothing in the Bible to indicate it. Circumcision was as a sign of a covenant, which brought only curses if not followed by the individual keeping the Law. Most of the Protestant reformers equated infant baptism with circumcision, but recognized its uselessness if not accompanied by a spiritual transformation made evident in the life of the individual.

Old Testament and New Testament Sacrifice

A sacrifice is the means by which a lesser person appeals to a greater person to not enforce a condition previously set by the greater person. The sacrifice is not only payment for an offence, but also represents the fact that the offence will no longer continue. On the basis of the sacrifice, the two persons can have fellowship, since the sacrifice establishes a covenant whereby the lesser person submits to the will of the greater person.

In Old Testament sacrifice, "It appears that before entering into communion with the Lord, sin had to be dealt with, then the burnt offering indicated the total consecration of the offerer to the Lord, and finally communion was possible."[6]

In New Testament sacrifice, the same reasons exist. "In both covenants, the ultimate requirement is a total sacrifice of one's self in humility before God's great work of objective atonement through the life that is in the sacrificial blood. Both a perfect blood sacrifice and a perfect sacrifice of love and allegiance to God were found in Christ, bringing an end to the forward look of the Levitical system."[7]

A sacrifice means nothing if the person in need of the sacrifice doesn't die to sin along with the sacrifice.

Under the Old Covenant, if a man had sex with a woman other than his wife, he might go to the Temple and slit the throat of an innocent lamb as a sacrifice for sin. Onlookers, not knowing what the sacrifice was for, would naturally assume the man was asking God to accept the life of the lamb in exchange for his own life. They knew the man needed to identify with the sacrifice as it died so the sin of the man would die along with the innocent animal.

The sacrifice was effective only if the external death was matched by an inward death to sin. But what if the man knew he was going to have sex that night with the same woman? Would God accept the sacrifice? "Hath the Lord as great delight in burnt offerings and sacrifices, as in obeying the voice of the Lord? Behold, to obey is better than sacrifice, and to hearken than the fat of rams. For rebellion is as the sin of witchcraft, and stubbornness is as iniquity and idolatry" (1 Samuel 15:22-23).

An Apology, the Modern Sacrifice

The following is an example of an effective modern sacrifice. Imagine you're standing in a long line at the supermarket. After ten minutes, you're just about to get to the checkout stand when a man cuts in front of you.

"Hey, get to the back of the line," you say.

"Oh, I'm sorry, I didn't realize there was a line," he says as he walks to the back of the line.

"That's OK." You accept his apology.

What just happened was a sin against you (cutting in front), a sacrifice offered with repentance (he apologized and went to the back of the line) and acceptance of the sacrifice (you accepted the apology and didn't hit the guy).

Again, the same scenario, but with different results:

"Hey, get to the back of the line," you say.

"Oh, I'm sorry, I didn't realize there was a line," the man says, but doesn't move an inch.

"Hey, I said go to the back of the line."

"Oh, I'm sorry, I didn't realize there was a line," he repeats—without moving.

What just happened was a sin against you (cutting in front), a sacrifice offered *without* repentance (he apologized, but didn't go to the back of the line) and no acceptance of the sacrifice (you can't accept the apology because it wasn't with repentance, so now you might hit the guy).

An apology, a modern day sacrifice, isn't effective without repentance. *Repentance means identifying with the sacrifice.* Unless the sacrifice represents a change on the inside, it's worse than useless.

Baptism Emblematic and Embodiment of Salvation

There is no doubt that early Christians were baptized because they "believed on the Lord Jesus Christ." Believing on His
sacrifice meant identifying with it ... the old man of sin dying on
the cross with Christ. Their faith assured them the same Spirit who
raised Christ from the dead would give them power over sin, so their
repentance was not in vain. Contained within baptism are most aspects of salvation, including belief, repentance, trust and assurance,
commitment and allegiance, and incorporation into Christian community.

As J.I. Packer wrote, "Christian baptism ... is a sign from
God that signifies inward cleansing from sins (Acts 22:16; 1 Corinthians 6:11; Ephesians 5:25-27), Spirit-wrought regeneration and
new life (Titus 3:5), and the abiding presence of God's Spirit as
God's seal testifying and guaranteeing that one will be kept safe in
Christ forever (1 Corinthians 12:13; Ephesians 1:13-14). Baptism
carries these meanings because first and fundamentally it signifies
union with Christ in His death, burial, and resurrection (Romans
6:3-7; Colossians 2:11-12); *and this union with Christ is the source
of every element in our salvation* (1 John 5:11-12)."[8] (my italics)

Stephen J. Wellum makes the case that baptism diminishes
in importance as philosophical pluralism increases. "A process, ex-
perts tell us, that does not necessarily lead to the abolition of God,
but rather to His marginalization in all aspects of our lives. Thus,
what is no longer central to us and what no longer drives us to our
knees and out to the world is the glory of God and the Gospel ...
when the burning realities of the Gospel are far from us ... is it any
wonder that baptism ... fades in its importance and significance?"[9]

What does it mean to "believe on the Lord Jesus Christ"? All
that is contained in baptism and more.

Church People Get Saved

Before psychology had become the explanation and answer for the human condition, there was a healthy debate regarding the claims of the born-again experience. Today, the presumption is, if there is a born-again experience, it's a wholly psychological process, with no influence from an outside force (i.e., the Holy Spirit), and therefore, subject to the claims of science.

It has not always been this way. Here's an excerpt from a book written in 1910 by a secular social reformer on the changes in prisoners who'd been born again:

"The evidence for the reality of these immense changes in character is overwhelming, and the only point where the psychologists find themselves at issue is the means by which they have been accomplished ... conversion is the only means by which a radically bad person can be changed into a radically good person. ... It produces not a change, but a revolution in character. It does not alter, it creates a new personality. Men who have been irretrievably bad, and under conversion have become ardent savers of the lost, tell us, with all the pathetic emphasis or their inexpressible and impenetrable discovery, that in the change that overcame them, they were conscious of being 'born again.'"[1]

Examine Yourselves

"Examine yourselves, whether ye be in the faith; prove your own selves. Know ye not your own selves, how that Jesus Christ is in you, except ye be reprobates?" (2 Corinthians 13:5).

"Give diligence to make your calling and election sure" (2 Peter 1:10).

Every pastor should ask his congregation, "Was there ever a time in your life when you knew absolutely that God was working in you, helping you to overcome sin? Have you ever experienced the workings of the Holy Spirit? Have you ever known righteousness, and peace, and joy in the Holy Ghost? (Romans 14:17). Have you enjoyed the Holy Spirit in your heart, crying 'Abba Father?' (Galatians

4:6). Have *you* ever enjoyed crying 'Abba Father' because of that same Spirit? (Romans 8:15). If not, I wonder if you are saved."

Most pastors don't want to question the salvation of their flock, preferring to teach them how to think and act like Christians.

But heathen don't have the Holy Spirit in them. As Finney said, "When people talk about conversion as a progressive work, they show that they know just as much about regeneration or conversion as Nicodemus did. They know nothing about what they should know, and are no better able to advise awakened sinners than Nicodemus was."[2]

We need to identify those who are not Christian, and show them the way of salvation. (see Appendices C, D, E and F)

When church people get saved, they usually have a testimony that includes the following:

1. They previously *assumed* they were saved because they went forward in an altar call and repeated a salvation prayer. After they are *truly* born again, they say the difference is like night and day.
2. They now know for the first time in their lives supernatural power over sin and experience righteousness, peace and joy in the Holy Ghost (Romans 14:17).
3. They are willing to tell their congregations about the definite difference between *thinking* you're saved and *experiencing* salvation.
4. They might challenge your church members to examine themselves against the two yardsticks of salvation: power over sin and the workings of the Holy Spirit within.
5. They might become so excited that they drag sinners into church, because for for the first time in their lives, they *know* the answer to *all* problems lies in relationship with Jesus Christ.

So perhaps getting your congregation saved is not that hard after all. Teach the two evidences of salvation and see a few of your members get saved, then let *them* tell the rest of the congregation. If you had five or six of these saints in your church, you might just have the beginnings of revival!

A Call to Action

I don't want to be overly dramatic, but burning in hell for all eternity is the *one* subject that shouldn't be taken lightly.

Forgive me if I offend with what I'm about to say.

When the world first learned of the systematic destruction of Jews in the 1940s, there were three responses that said a great deal about the way man rationalizes inactivity when faced with unthinkable reality.

The first response was, "I don't believe it," and the people did nothing. The second response was, "I can't do anything about it," and the people did nothing. A third response was perhaps the most hideous. Some theologians taught it was rebellion against God to resist Hitler.

As horrible as the holocaust was, it pales in comparison to the possibility that 100 million Americans think they are going to heaven because they repeated a salvation prayer.

But because we can't hear screams and smell burning flesh, we're tempted to leave well enough alone. After all, most 20th century ministers adopted Billy Sunday's methods and theology, so who are *we* to rock the boat? How could they *all* be wrong, and besides, God wouldn't let us stray so far from the truth.

This was the way many Catholic priests rationalized doing nothing when confronted with Luther's *95 Thesis*. Surely the Pope and *almost all* theologians couldn't be wrong! These people love God after all. They've given their lives to His service. God wouldn't allow such a deception!

Reformation

Evangelical Christianity is facing it's biggest challenge since the fourth century. Most Protestants call the time from Constantine to Luther "the dark ages" because saving faith was not taught correctly. America has entered it's own dark age. *It's time for another reformation.*

FOOTNOTES:

Introduction
1. Dr. James Dobson, *Focus on the Family Newsletter* (October, 1990), p.3
2. Ibid.
3. See Chapter, *General Hospital*
4. *Southern Baptist Council 2002 Annual Meeting*
5. David Frost, Personal thought of a Public Man, (1997), p. 72
6. David W. Bercot, *Will The Real Heretics Stand Up* (1999), p.129
7. Dr. R. L. Hymers, *The Church That Will be Left Behind* (2001), p. 3
8. Luis Palau, *The Only Hope For America* (1996), p. 10
9. James Dobson, *Focus On The Family Newsletter* (August, 1998), p. 2
10. Bill Bright, *Red Sky In The Morning* (1998), p. 212

The Front Page
1. Ray Comfort and Kirk Cameron, *The School Of Biblical Evangelism,* (2004), p. 133
2. Ray Comfort and Kirk Cameron, *The Way Of The Master,* (2004), pp. 61-64

The faith System
1. John Dillenberger and Claude Welch, *Protestant Christianity,* (1958), pp. 271-272
2. Phillip S. Watson, *The Message Of The Wesleys* (1984), p. 163
3. Ibid., p. 125
4. Franklin Graham, *Rebel With A Cause*, (1995), p.120
5. Ibid., p. 122
6. Ibid., pp. 122,123
7. John Pollock, *Billy Graham* (1966), p. 251
8. Ibid., p. 104
9. Billy Graham, "Evangelism, Message And Method," *Christianity Today* (August, 1959)
10. John Pollock, *Billy Graham* (1966), p. 134
11. George Barna, *State Of The Church 2002*, (2002), p. 114

General Hospital
1. George Barna, *State Of The Church 2002*, (2002), p. 66
2. Ibid., p. 98
3. Ibid., p. 97
4. Ibid., pp. 127-128
5. Ibid., p. 128
6. Ibid., pp. 95-97
7. Ibid., p. 114
8. See chapter, *Edwards, Whitefield and Wesley*
9. George Barna, *State Of The Church 2002,* (2002), p. 125

A Funny Thing Happened on the way to the Temple
1. H. D. McDonald, *Salvation*, (1982), p. 150
2. Kirk Cameron & Ray Comfort, *The School Of Biblical Evangelism*, (2004), p.21

The Hour Of Decision

1. David Bennett, *The Altar Call,* (2000), pp 171-172
2. Ibid
3. Colin Marshall, *Time Is Now Video,* (1994) , session 4
4 Rev. E.J.Goodspeed, D.D., *Moody and Sankey in America,* (1876), p.440
5. David Bennett, *The Altar Call,* (2000), pp 194
6. Moody, John Pollock, (1984) pp. 111,112
7. Rev. E. J. Goodspeed, D.D., *Moody and Sankey in Great Britain and America,* (1876), p. 441
8. John MacArthur Jr., *The Gospel According to Jesus,* (1994), p 29
9. Ibid

Edward, Whitefield and Wesley

1. "Definite and complete" includes not only a definite and complete atonement, but also the indwelling of the Holy Spirit and the supernatural impartation of a new nature which overcomes the old nature. "Lack of sanctification" was never used as an excuse for backsliding. Sanctification was always taught as a going forward from "glory to glory." No pre-20th century evangelist would ever say a person was backslidden if they never showed any sign of having forslidden. They would be told they were never saved.
2. Harry S. Stout, *The Divine Dramatist,* (1991), p. 39
3. Sermon, "*Other Sheep and One Flock*"
4. Harry S. Stout, *The Divine Dramatist,* (1991), p. 39
5. Ibid
6. *Jonathan Edwards Basic Writings,* (1966), p. XVIII
7. See footnote 1
8. *Jonathan Edwards Basic Writings,* (1966), p. XVIII
9. Harry S. Stout, *The Divine Dramatist,* (1991), p.39
10. Erroll Hulse, *The Great Invitation,* (1986), pp. 142-143
11. Ibid., p. 141

Charles Finney

1. John Dillenberger and Claude Welch, *Protestant Christianity,* (1958), p. 166
2. Ibid., p170
3. Ibid., p. 21
4. Charles Finney, *Lectures on Revivals* (1988), pp. 18-19
5. "It is marvellous credulity, to take every excitement in the name of religion, for the work of God's Spirit. It is an enormous demand on our charity, when we are asked in mass, as true and solid, the wholesale conversions that are made in this way." Rev. J. W. Nevin, D.D. *The Anxious Bench* (1843), p. 12
6. Ibid., p. 13
7. Henry B. McLendon, *The Mourner's Bench* (1902), p. 45
8. Ichabod Spencer, *A Pastor's Sketches,* (2002) pp.107-109
9. Rev. J. W. Nevin, D.D., *The Anxious Bench* (1843), p. 21

Billy Sunday Changes Everything

1. Elijah P. Brown, *The Real Billy Sunday* (1914), p. 146
2. Original Source Newspaper, 1918

3. Lyle W. Dorsett, *Billy Sunday, The Redemption of Urban America* (1991), p. 136
4. William G. McLoughlin, Jr., *Billy Sunday Was His Real Name* (1955), p. 102
5. Lyle W. Dorsett, *Billy Sunday* (1991), p. 136
6. John Pollock, *Moody* (1997), p. 201
7. Ibid., p. 251
8. *International Standard Bible Encyclopedia,* (1979) p.768 Vol I
9. Oswald Chambers, *My Utmost For His Highest,* (1946), p. 10
10. G. Campbell Morgan, D.D, *Evangelism,* (1903), pp. 83-85
11. Original Source Sunday Organization Document, (1918)
12. Joel A. Carpenter, *The Youth For Christ Movement and It's Pioneers*, (1988) P. 28
13. William T. Ellis, *Billy Sunday, The Man and His Message,* (1936, p.14
14.. Lyle W. Dorsett, *Billy Sunday,* (1991) p.108
15. Original source report from Moody Church, 1918
16. Roger A. Bruns, *Preacher Billy Sunday and Big-Time Evangelism,* (1992), p.76
17. G. B. F. Hallock, *The Evangelist Encyclopedia*, (1930), p. 255

Billy Sunday Evangelism Evolves
1. Douglas W. Frank, *Less Than Conquerers*, (1986), pp.206-208
2. Ibid., p.176
3. Ibid.
4. William G. McLoughlin, Jr., *Billy Sunday Was His Real Name* (1955), p. 43
5. Billy Sunday, *Sermon transcript, April 15, 1917 Afternoon*, p.33, Box 6, Reel 9, Sunday Papers
6. Billy Sunday, *Sermon transcript, New York, May 27, 1917 Afternoon*, p.5, Box 8, Reel 11, Sunday Papers
7. Theodore Thomas Frankenberg, *The Spectacular Career Of Reverend Billy Sunday*, p.213
8. *Doctrines and Disciplines of the Salvation Army*, (1881)
9. William G. McLoughlin, Jr., *Billy Sunday Was His Real Name*, (1955), p.128
10. Ibid.
11. Betty Lee Skinner, *Daws* p. 37
12. Ibid., p. 56
13. Dawson Trotman, *Born To Reproduce Tract,* pp. 40-41
14. Ibid., p. 70
15. Betty Lee Skinner, *Daws*, p. 26
16. John Pollock, *Billy Graham* (1966), p. 251
17. Betty Lee Skinner, *Daws*, p. 70
18. Bill Bright, *Red Sky In The Morning,* p. 205
19. A. W. Tozer, *I Call It Heresy*, (1974), p.9
20. Paris Reidhead, *Getting Evangelicals Saved,*(1989), p. 46
21. Michael Richardson, *Amazing Faith*, (2000), pp. 221
22. Ibid., p. 34
23. Ibid., p. 23
24. Bill Bright, *Come Help Change the World*, Here's Life Publishers, 1985, pp. 28-29
25. Charles Finney, *Lectures on revival*, (1988), p.211
26.   Jonathan Edwards, *An Humble Inquiry into the Rules of the Word of God, concerning the Qualifications requisite to a Complete Standing and Full Communion in the Visible Church of God*

Visible Church of God
27. Bill Bright, *Four Spiritual Laws Tract*
28. Jonathan Edwards, *The Works Of Jonathan Edwards,* (1979), p. 237
29. Michael Richardson, *Amazing Faith,* (2000), pp. 221
30. Ibid., pp. 139

The Billy Graham Formula
1."Reverend Billy Graham talking with David Frost," PBS, January 23, 1993 as recorded in David Frost's *Billy Graham - Personal Thoughts of a Public Man,* (1997), pp.71-72
2. John Pollock, *Billy Graham* (1966), p. 251
3. Ibid., p.165
4. "Reverend Billy Graham talking with David Frost," PBS, January 23, 1993 as recorded in David Frost's *Billy Graham - Personal Thoughts of a Public Man,* (1997), pp.71-72
5. Curtis Mitchell, *Those Who Came Forward*, (1966), p.40-41
6. John Pollock, *Billy Graham* (1966), p. 104
7. Ibid., p.165
8. Betty Lee Skinner, *Daws*, p. 117
9. John Pollock, *Billy Graham* (1966), p. 134
10. Ibid.
11. Ibid., p. 104
12. John Pollock, *Billy Graham,* (1966), pp.103-104
13. Betty Lee Skinner, *Daws*, p. 117
14. Billy Graham, *Peace With God*, (1955), p. 111
15. Ibid
16. John Pollock, *Billy Graham,* (1966), pp.107-108
17. Curtis Mitchell, *Those Who Came Forward*, (1966), p.45
18. John Pollock, *Billy Graham,* (1966), pp.108
19. Ibid., pp.103-104
20. Curtis Mitchell, *Those Who Came Forward*, (1966), p.41
21. Ibid.
22 John Pollock, *Billy Graham,* (1966), p.108
23. Ibid., p. 104
24. Curtis Mitchell, *Those Who Came Forward*, (1966), p.40-41
25. John Pollock, *Billy Graham,* (1966), pp.191
26. Charisma Editorial, (July, 2005), p.6
27. David Lockard, *The Unheard Billy Graham*, (1971), p.54
28. Curtis Mitchell, *Those Who Came Forward*, (1966), p.25
29. John Pollock, *Billy Graham,* (1966), pp.109
30. Ibid., pp.133-134
31. Stanley N. Gundry, *Love Them In, The Life And Theology of D. L. Moody*, (1996), p.82
32. Curtis Mitchell, *Those Who Came Forward*, (1966), p.11

The Evangelical Sacrament
1. John Wesley White, *What Does It Mean To Be Born Again?*, (1977) pp.43,44
2. Ibid., p.44

Billy Sunday Evangelism Hits the Fan
1. *Charles Spurgeon sermon* (1627)
2. Charles Finney, *Lectures on Revivals* (1988), pp. 227-228
3. Ibid., p. 238
4. Ibid., p. 233

The Bride of Christ
1. E. M. B. Green, *The Meaning Of Salvation* (1965), Pg 166
2. Heinrich Baltensweiler, *The New International Dictionary of New Testament Theology, Volume 1,* (1986), p. 560

What do you think I am, a Saint?
1. David bennett, *The Altar Call*, (2000) p. 138
2. Ibid., p. 135
3. Charles Finney, *Lectures on Revivals* (1988), p. 76
4. Henry Bettenson, ed., *Documents Of The Christian Church* (1963), p. 186
5. Martin Luther, *Luther's Works*, Volume 25, (1972), pp. 322-326
6. Ligonier Ministries, *Tabletalk*, (May, 1991)
7. Founders Journal, *The Lordship Controversy and The Carnal Christian Teaching* (Part 1), Issue 16

What does it mean to Believe on the Lord Jesus Christ?
1. Gordan T. Smith, *Beginning Well*, (20010, p.145
2. E. M. B. Green, *The Meaning Of Salvation* (1965), Pg 170-171
3. Matthew Henry, *Electronic Database - Biblesoft,* (2002) 1 Peter 3-4
4. Barnes Notes, *Electronic Database - Biblesoft,* (2002) 1 Peter 3-4
5. Jamieson, Fausset, and Brown, *Electronic Database - Biblesoft,* (2002), 1 Peter 3-4
6. *The International Standard Bible Encyclopedia* Volume 4 (1988), p. 1272
7. Ibid.
8. J. I. Packer, *Concise Theology,* (1993), p.212
9. Stephen J. Wellum, *The Compromised Church,* (1998), p. 152

Church People Get Saved
1. Harold Begbie, *Twice Born Men. A Clinic In Regeneration* (1910), pp. 17-18
2. Charles Finney, *Lectures on revival,* (1988), p. 211

Appendices

1. Phillip S. Watson, *The Message Of The Wesleys* (1984), pp. 131-133
2. Charles Finney, *Lectures on Revival* (1988), Pg 207-224
3. Ibid., pp. 225-236
4. Charles Finney, *Lectures To Professing Christians,* Lecture 1(1837)

Appendix A
Evangelism Timeline

1740: Edwards, Whitefield and Wesley

Born-again experience separated from local church membership. Whitefield and Wesley never used altar calls. Prayer and counseling was offered to inquirers seeking salvation. Perhaps 5 percent of those who stayed for prayer were "hopefully saved." No "salvation prayer" was ever used. Evidence of salvation was power over sin and workings of the Holy Spirit in the individual. Inquirers were not told they were saved.

1830: Finney

Finney used methods that evolved into the altar call to encourage inquirers to repent. After-meetings were offered for those seeking salvation. Perhaps 5 to 10 percent of those who stayed for prayer were "hopefully saved." No "salvation prayer" was ever used. Evidence of salvation was power over sin and workings of the Holy Spirit in the individual. Inquirers were not told they were saved.

1910: Sunday

Salvation paradigm was completely changed by Sunday. All inquirers were told they were saved. Inquiry room was eliminated. No after- meeting offered for those seeking salvation. One hundred percent of those who shook Sunday's hand and signed a *Convert's Pledge* were converts. Evidence of salvation no longer an issue. "Sunday Convert" becomes a term of derision.

1955: Graham

Graham instituted three-part formula for success including bringing back the inquiry room, the after-meeting, extensive counseling and extensive follow-up programs. Graham introduced the group salvation prayer.

TODAY: Thousand of Ministers

Using only a sermon and Graham's group salvation prayer, today's ministers generate perhaps 90 percent false conversions.

Appendix B
Two Doctrines That Helped Effective Evangelism

The Beneficial Influence of the Calvinist Doctrine of Pre-faith "Regeneration"

Since Billy Sunday, respect for the invisible work of God in the pre-faith penitent has been largely ignored. Before 1910, evangelists of the Calvinist persuasion used methods that worked in concert with the doctrine of pre-faith regeneration, but now most non-Arminian ministers ignore this perspective and choose instead to proclaim almost universal salvation for all who come to the altar. (Please be aware that both "monergistic"–God applies irresistible grace to man–and "synergistic"–man allows God to change him–regeneration are equally de-emphasized by modern evangelism.)

This doctrine of pre-faith regeneration was the main reason most clergy were so against the public preaching outside the walls of a church building of Whitefield, Wesley, and all subsequent evangelists up until Finney. Although they were wrong to fault public preaching, the very thing they feared has come to pass. Confusion is epidemic in modern Christianity. Over 60 percent of Americans say they are Christian because they have "said a prayer that is still significant to them today." According to the latest polling data on what Americans believe, less than 10 percent could be called Christian in the biblical sense.

For Calvinists, the understanding of pre-faith regeneration guided the altar call, making it an appeal for further inquiry into the condition of the penitent rather than the conclusion of a contract. (In fact, modern evangelists see the altar call and the repeating of a salvation prayer the way the early church saw water baptism.)

Have you ever heard a modern evangelist caution a penitent that he should never say a salvation prayer unless he personally knows what God expects of him? For the Calvinist, this would be a call for self-examination (2 Corinthians 13:5), to see if Christ had illuminated the penitent enough to make a public profession of faith. In fact, evangelists before Billy Sunday never led anyone in a salvation prayer for the obvious reason that, if a person had to be led by an evangelist, then the Holy Spirit had not illuminated the penitent enough for him to say his own unique prayer from the heart. In fact, if God has done His work, the penitent could not be constrained from saying a salvation prayer since his entire being would cry, "Hosanna!"

Before 1910, the Calvinist evangelist saw the workings of God with the penitent as a courtship of Christ with his bride. God woos the bride, tells her He loves her and explains all the things He's going to do for her if she yields completely. As the bride yields, God imparts deep spiritual truths, revealing sin for what it is. As the bride yields further, God finally cleanses her of all sin, making the public profession of faith (the marriage ceremony) only a reflection of the salvation that has already been accomplished.

Calvinists used to see the public profession of faith, "If you confess with your mouth Jesus [as] Lord," as an obvious result of having already believed "in your heart that God raised Him from the dead." Now the understanding of the sequence of salvation is all muddled. If you were to ask the typical non-Arminian church member when they were saved, they would say it was when they went to the altar and repeated a salvation prayer.

The Calvinist evangelist before Billy Sunday acted as God's best man (2 Corinthians 11:2), extolling the virtues of the Bridegroom to the bride, explaining the virtues of marriage to the Holy God, explaining to the bride she must be submitted in all things to her spiritual husband. He understood the personal and delicate love relationship between the betrothed and Christ and heeded the Bridegroom's admonition, "I adjure you, O daughters of Jerusalem, by the gazelles or by the hinds of the field, that you will not arouse or awaken my love, until she pleases" (Song of Songs 2:7 NASB).

This beautiful romance can be pre-empted and even destroyed by the coarse intervention of a meddler. For the modern evangelist to present salvation as a "one size fits all" faith product is an offense to Him who is LOVE. It denigrates the courtship of God with His beloved and cheapens salvation to the place where it ceases to be effective for the majority of people who go to the altar.

The Beneficial Influence of the Arminian Doctrine of Pre-faith "Awakening"

The Arminian doctrine of pre-faith awakening is just as essential to effective evangelism for the Arminians as the Calvinist doctrine of pre-faith regeneration is for the Calvinists. You probably know that Whitefield and Wesley were equally devoted to God, but they were on opposite sides of the pre-faith issue. But who can say Wesley was any less effective an evangelist than Whitefield? If you examine the two pre-faith doctrines, you will find their beneficial effect on evangelism is identical.

Both Whitefield and Wesley had pre-faith experiences. Like Luther before them, the pre-faith illumination of the two men drove them to seek God's complete salvation. In the case of Whitefield, he was illumined by the Holy Spirit sufficiently to attempt to serve God with his whole being (as much as was possible before regeneration). All the time he fasted and did good works, he knew he wasn't saved.

Wesley was in a similar pitiful state. He met with Whitefield in the pre-dawn hours seeking God's face in what became known as "The Holy Club." They fasted and prayed that God would "break through" with His salvation. (There is not a prominent evangelist today who wouldn't have accepted these lost men unreservedly as brothers–how shallow and superficial is our Christianity.) Wesley went to the colonies to work among the native Americans. After three years, he came back an utter failure. He said in the hull of the boat on its way back to England, "I went to America to convert the Indians; but O! who shall convert me?"

Whitefield and Wesley experienced with Luther what every person must experience for himself–the Holy Spirit's illumination of sin, the schoolmaster of the Law and the sorrow that leads to repentance. And in these steps of divine intervention, all three recognized the sovereignty of God as an integral part of the salvation process. These most beloved men of God could not force His hand. God knew the exact moment to save them for the maximum benefit to His Kingdom and the prosperity of the saints.

Appendix C
Wesley's Waiting on God For Salvation (excerpts)
The Means of Grace

Wesley discusses what the believer (who is not yet born again) can do while waiting for God to save him:

It cannot possibly be conceived that the word of God should give no direction in so important a point. ... We have only to consult the oracles of God, inquire what is written there ... all who desire the grace of God are to wait for it in the means which he hath ordained; in using, not in laying them aside.

But what are the steps which Scriptures direct us to take, in the working out of our own salvation? The Prophet Isaiah gives us a general answer, touching the first steps which we are to take; 'cease to do evil: learn to do well.'

If ever you desire that God should work in you that faith whereof cometh both present and eternal salvation, by the grace already given fly from all sin as from the face of a serpent; carefully avoid every evil word and work; yea, abstain from all appearance of evil. And 'learn to do well.'

Be zealous of good works, of works of piety as well as of works of mercy; family prayer, and crying to God in secret. Fast in secret, and 'your father that seeth in secret, he will reward you openly.' 'Search the Scriptures': hear them in public, read them in private, and meditate therein ...

Baptism is an outward sign of an inward grace. ... I tell the sinner, 'you must be born again.' 'No,' say you; 'he was born again in baptism. Therefore he cannot be born again now.' Alas what trifling is this! ... Therefore do not play upon words. He must go through an entire change of heart ... if either he or you die without it, your baptism will be so far from profiting you that it will greatly increase your damnation.[1]

Appendix D
Finney's False Comfort for Sinners (excerpts)

(On Repentance)

Now the object of instructing an anxious sinner should be to lead him by the shortest possible way to do this. It is to bring his mind, by the shortest route, to the practical conclusion that there is, in fact, no other way in which he can be relieved and saved, but to renounce himself and rest in Christ alone. To do this with effect requires great skill. It requires a thorough knowledge of the human heart, a clear understanding of the plan of salvation, and a precise and definite idea of the very thing that a sinner must do in order to be saved.

To know how to do this effectually is one of the rarest qualifications in the ministry at the present day. It is distressing to see how few ministers, and how few professors of religion there are who have in their own minds that distinct idea of the thing to be done, that they can go to an anxious sinner and tell him exactly what he has to do, and how to do it, and can show him clearly that there is no possible way for him to be saved but by doing that very thing which they tell him, and can make him feel the certainty that he must do it, and that unless he does that very thing, he will be damned.

(On true compassion for sinners)

The direct object of many persons is to comfort sinners, and they are often so intent upon this that they do not stick at means or kind of comfort. They see their friends distressed, and they pity them, they feel very compassionate, "Oh, oh, I cannot bear to see them so distressed, I must comfort them somehow," and so they try one way, and another, and all to comfort them! Now, God desires they should be comforted. He is benevolent, and has kind feelings, and his heart yearns over them, when he sees them so distressed. But he sees that there is only one way to give a sinner real comfort. He has more benevolence and compassion than all men, and wishes to comfort them. But he has fixed the terms as unyielding as his throne, on which he will give a sinner relief. And he will not alter. He knows that nothing else will do the sinner effectual good, for nothing can make him happy, until he repents of his sins and forsakes them, and turns to God. And therefore God will not yield.

Our object should be the same as that of God. We should feel compassion and benevolence, just as he does, and be as ready to give comfort, but be sure that it be of the right kind. The fact is, our prime object should be to induce the sinner to obey God. His comfort ought to be with us, and with him, but a secondary object, and while we are more anxious to relieve his distress than to have him cease to abuse, and dishonor God, we are not likely, by our instructions, to do him any real good.

(On Regeneration)

Regeneration–which we also call conversion–is not a progressive work. What is regeneration but the beginning of obedience to God? How can a beginning be progressive? Regeneration is the first act of genuine obedience to God, the first voluntary action of the mind that God approves. That is conversion. When people talk about conversion as a progressive work, they show that they know just as much about regeneration or conversion as Nicodemus did. They know nothing about what they should know, and are no better to advise awakened sinners than Nicodemus was.

(On allowing seekers to suffer)

"The sinner has reason for distress, because he doesn't have any Christian faith. If he had God with him he wouldn't feel awful. If he were a Christian he would rejoice. But to tell an unrepentant sinner to be cheerful? You might as well preach in hell, "Cheer up! Don't feel bad." The sinner totters on the verge of hell. He rebels against God and his peril is infinitely greater than he thinks. What a doctrine of demons–to tell a hellish rebel not to get worked up! What causes his distress but his own rebellion? He isn't comforted because he refuses comfort. God wants to relieve him, more passionately than does any human being. The instant the sinner submits to Christ, God's comfort will overwhelm him.

(On how to work with seekers–a useful guide for altar calls)

Christians, never tell a sinner anything or direct him to do anything that will stop him short of absolute submission to God. Suppose you tell an unbeliever to pray or to read or to do anything less than saving repentance, and that night he falls and breaks his neck. Whom will God blame? It makes the hearts of the faithful bleed to see how many people delude anxious sinners. Their answers are false. What vast spiritual quackery we see in the world— what liars and worthless spiritual doctors who prescribe only false hopes. They dispense false tenderness because they lack firmness to apply the sword of the spirit to cut men and women to the soul, to expose sinners' naked hearts. Many who enter the ministry lack enough skill to administer the Gospel, and enough firmness to watch as God's Spirit crushed rotten hopes until the sinner breaks at the feet of Christ.[2]

Appendix E
Finney's Directions to Sinners (excerpts)

(On repentance)

Many think remorse, a sense of guilt, is repentance. Then hell is full of repentance, because it is full of unutterable, eternal remorse. Others feel regret over something and call that repentance. But they regret their sin because of the consequences, not because they hate sin. This isn't repentance.

(On false Christians)

I know some people who claim to be Christians who would be full of glee to run back to their old ways, if they didn't fear ruining their reputation. ... But listen: If they feel that way they have no claim to be Christians; they don't hate sin. If they long for their old ways, they show they have never really repented, because repentance always consists in changing views and feelings. If they were truly converted, instead of desiring such things, they would turn from them with loathing.

(On faith)

Faith isn't an intellectual conviction for the world's sins—or even for you in particular—nor is it a belief that you are a Christian or that your sins are forgiven. Rather, faith is that trust in the Scriptures that leads a person to act as if they are true.

(On living for God)

Giving your heart to God is the same thing as giving it to anybody else. ... it means to set my affections on Him and strive to please Him in everything. True submission is obeying God. ... He must cease striving against his maker and take the attitude of an obedient child, willing to be and do whatever God requires.

(On what to tell sinners)

Call sinners to choose whether they will serve God or the world, whether they will follow holiness or sin. Make them understand what it means to choose, and what they should choose. If they answer from the heart they will be saved.[3]

Appendix F
Finney's True and False Conversions (excerpts)

An individual who is converted is benevolent, and not supremely selfish. ... This is God's state of mind ... that true conversion is a change from a state of supreme selfishness to benevolence. *It is a change in the end of pursuit, and not a mere change in the means of attaining the end. ... The true and the false convert differ in this. The true convert chooses, as the end of his pursuit, the glory of God and the good of his kingdom. This end he chooses for its own sake, because he views this as the greatest good, as a greater good than his own individual happiness.*

(True and false converts)

Both may pay equal regard to what is right; the true convert because he loves what is right, and the other because he knows he cannot be saved unless he does right. He is honest in his common business transactions, because it is the only way to secure his own interest. Verily, they have their reward. They get the reputation of being honest among men, but *if they have no higher motive, they will have no reward from God.*

To repent. The true convert abhors sin on account of its hateful nature, because it dishonors God, and therefore he desires to repent of it. The other desires to repent, because he knows that unless he does repent he will be damned.

To believe in Jesus Christ. The true saint desires it to glorify God, and because he loves the truth for its own sake. The other desires to believe, that he may have a stronger hope of going to heaven.

To obey God. The true saint that he may increase in holiness; the false professor because he desires the rewards of obedience.

They may both design to be truly holy; the true saint because he loves holiness, and the deceived person because he knows that he can be happy in no other way.

Both may love the society of the saints; the true convert because his soul enjoys their spiritual conversation, the other because he hopes to derive some advantage from their company.

They may both love the doctrines of grace, the true saint be-
cause they are so glorious to God, the other because he thinks them
a guarantee of his own salvation.

The deceived person has only a purpose of obedience, and
the other has a preference of obedience. The true saint ... really
prefers, and in his heart chooses obedience, and therefore he finds it
easy to obey.

The true convert and the deceived person also differ in their
faith. The true saint has a confidence in the general character of
God, that leads him to unqualified submission to God. ... One child
obeys his parent from confidence in his parent. He has faith which
works by love. The other yields an outward obedience from hope
and fear.

The true convert has this faith, or confidence in God, that
leads him to obey God because he loves God. This is the obedi-
ence of faith. He has that confidence in God, that he submits himself
wholly into the hands of God.

The other has only a partial faith, and only a partial submission. The devil has a partial faith. He believes and trembles. A person may believe that Christ came to save sinners, and on that ground
may submit to him, to be saved; while he does not submit wholly
to him, to be governed and disposed of. *His submission is only on*
condition that he shall be saved. It is never with that unreserved
confidence in God's whole character, that leads him to say, "Let thy
will be done." He only submits to be saved. His religion is the religion of law. The other is gospel religion. One is selfish, the other
benevolent. Here lies the true difference between the two classes.
The religion of one is outward and hypocritical. The other is that of
the heart, holy, and acceptable to God.

OBJECTION: Do not the inspired writers say, Repent, and
believe the gospel, and you shall be saved?

ANSWER: Yes; but they require true repentance; that is, to
forsake sin because it is hateful in itself. *It is not true repentance, to*
forsake sin on condition of pardon, or to say, "I will be sorry for my
sins, if you will forgive me." So they require true faith, and true sub-
mission; not conditional faith, or partial submission. This is what

the Bible insists on.

OBJECTION: Does not the gospel hold out pardon as a motive to submission?

ANSWER: This depends on the sense in which you mean the term motive. If you mean that God spreads out before men his whole character, and the whole truth of the case, as reasons to engage the sinner's love and repentance, I say, Yes; his compassion, and willingness to pardon, are reasons for loving God, because they are a part of his glorious excellence, which we are bound to love. But *if you mean by motive a condition, and that the sinner is to repent on condition he shall be pardoned, then I say, that the Bible no where holds out any such view of the matter. It never authorizes a sinner to say, "I will repent if you will forgive," and no where offers pardon as a motive to repentance, in such a sense as this.*[4]

Author's note: Many readers will find Finney's explanations hard to understand since Western law is based on external adherence and not internal submission. But please examine every instance in the Bible where a person obeys the requirements of God only externally. These Jesus labeled as "hypocrites," which means "actors" in the Greek. Is there even one instance in the Bible where a hypocrite escapes the wrath of God? No. In fact, God condemns this group more vehemently than unrepentant sinners that are honest about their true condition (Revelation 3:16).

Some may point to water baptism and circumcision. These sacraments are external symbols of an inward grace. Without a commensurate heart, the candidate does nothing more than get wet or lose a little weight. In the case of infants, these ordinances are always done in the hope of future commitment to God. If the child grows up and shows no evidence of regeneration during his lifetime, the ordinance was obviously of no lasting effect except as a sign of parental devotion.

This is the way most evangelicals see water baptism and circumcision. I pray we start using the same standard for altar calls and "salvation prayers."

Appendix G
About the Author

When I was eleven years old, I went fishing in a stream that winds through the city of Buffalo, New York. I caught a large quantity of tiny fish. The fish were too small to eat, but that didn't change the fact that I caught more fish than any of my friends. If I had thrown the fish back, the fish would have grown bigger, but instead I threw them on the bank where they flopped until they died. When I got up to leave, since I had no use for the fish, I left them, hoping no one was looking.

When I was thirty-five years old, I went fishing for converts at a shopping mall in Bonita, California. A group from my church had gone out most every Saturday for over a year. Sometimes we went to the parks, sometimes door-to-door, sometimes to shopping malls. My particular group consisted of trained evangelists, having completed the *Glad Tidings Evangelism Course* and done many kinds of evangelism in the United States and Mexico. We had even established and nurtured a flourishing church in the slums outside Tijuana, Mexico.

We used a tract called *The Two Question Test*. We were trained to identify those people most likely to be receptive to a presentation of the Gospel. (Much of it has to do with practical considerations. For example, couples are more receptive than large groups.) We approached people with lead-in lines like, "I'm asking people if they'd like to take a test that shows whether they're going to go to heaven. Would you like to take the test? It only takes a few minutes."

I witnessed to a receptive eighteen-year-old boy. This kid would have done anything I asked. He answered all the questions correctly, indicating he understood the Gospel. I came to the end of the tract where I was supposed to lead him in a formula salvation prayer. It would have been so easy. And then I'd be able to tell the church, "We got another one saved." I hesitated. Just then a fellow evangelist came by and basically said I should get the decision, and, if I didn't, the boy might be hit by a car and his blood would be on my head. After all, "Now is the day of salvation." But I remembered my experience at the Spring Valley Swap Meet days before.

I used this same tract at swap meets (people back east call them flea markets) all over the San Diego area with great success–or so I thought at the time. I used to set up a ten-foot booth with a huge banner inviting shoppers to come and take the *Two Question Test* to find out if they were going to heaven when they died.

It was at the Spring Valley Swap Meet I had my first doubts about what I was doing. Six giggling Baptist girls (fourteen to nineteen years old) came into my booth thinking, I assume, they were going to have a good time with this young evangelist. I led them through the test and not one of them could tell me why they should go to heaven when they died. There were the usual "I try to be a good person" and "I keep the Ten Commandments," and "I go to church," etc., but when each of these reasons was discredited with scriptures, the girls couldn't come up with the correct answer.

I can't remember if I led them in a formula salvation prayer or just explained the Gospel to them and admonished them to completely turn their lives over to God. I wrestled with the realization that I was part of the problem. These six girls had gone forward in countless altar calls at church camps, revivals and youth meetings and still weren't saved. What possible purpose would there be in leading them in still another "salvation prayer" if the previous prayers had resulted in nothing more than the delusion that they were saved?

How many evangelists would question the salvation of six bright-eyed Baptists who thought they were born again? How could these girls go though life thinking they were saved when, at any moment, they could slip into a Christless eternity? Who's responsible? Who's to blame?

Since that day at the shopping mall in Bonita, California, I try to catch only the fish God gives me, and pray I never leave a fish on the riverbank to die.